MEET
GOD

MEET
GOD

AN INTRODUCTION TO
THE GOD OF THE BIBLE

Greg Carman

If you wish to contact Greg, he can be reached by:

Phone: 1-573-686-3923
Email: jamescarman53@gmail.com

Print information available on the last page.

Rev. date: 01/19/2021

To order additional copies of this book, contact:
Xlibris
844-714-8691
www.Xlibris.com
Orders@Xlibris.com
823537

CONTENTS

ACKNOWLEDGEMENTS

I know, at some level what I have written. I have no Idea what you will understand or take away from reading this book. That said, I believe it important to recognize those who have aided me in the 4 year effort you are reading today. I'll begin with Andy B. and Gerry C. Two brothers in Christ who listened to me explain about a message that was invading my thoughts on an increasing basis. At once and almost simultaneously they said, "sounds like you need to write a book". With this encouragement I began to comply having no idea what the end would be.

Next I owe a huge debt to Paul H. and Brian S. One a former minister and the other a current pastor. Both steeped in the word of God and willing to read and challenge my thinking in several areas of content. They both offered suggestions for accuracy and to improve the ease of reading this text.

I am also indebted to the many bible teachers, preachers, ministers, professors, editors, and evangelist I have been graced to hear over the past 60 years. My special thanks to Edward F., Leroy G., Terry R., Marvin P., Jim W., Patrick M., Seth M., Rick A., Brent S., Leamon F., and Ray C. There are too many to enumerate individually but these few stand out as having challenged and shaped my growth the past 40 years. God blessed them with amazing abilities to communicate Jesus in word and deed. Some have passed to their reward, and others have many lives yet to enlighten. May God continue to bless their ministries.

The author photo on the back cover was gracefully done by Chris P. a brother in Christ. Most of you will never know how little he had to work with, and yet he made me look good. Thanks, Chris.

Next is Karen, my friend, wife, and mother of our children. She exhibited a balanced amount of encouragement to write when I didn't feel like doing so and reminding me of the promise I made. Thank you honey, I am fairly sure I would still be on chapter one without your efforts.

Lastly, I thank God. As creator, Father, Son and Holy Spirit, they put me on this course, and I thank them for the learning and wisdom they shared with me as I reflected and struggled to complete this task. Any errors or misstatements within are mine and any glory to be given, belongs solely to HIM.

Foreword

Throughout the centuries, there has been an ebb and flow of knowledge about the God of scripture. Revival occurs periodically, increasing the curiosity of many, but over time, it wanes, and ignorance prevails. (Those who experienced the terrorist act of "9/11" will also remember the talk of prayer, questions of "Why did God allow . . .," and the increase of church attendance for a few months.)

The purpose of the book is to restore information as to the nature, characteristics, qualities, and attributes of God, a.k.a. Yahweh.

The goal is to enlighten those who have never been taught about the Living God, also those who have been lulled into a myopic view of God as one- or two-dimensional in nature.

The hope is to stir a sense of urgency to seek and find this most important entity in existence. This is the author's attempt to inform the reader about the God of the Bible with easily understood explanations of who, what, where, when, and how of the eternal. There will also be a modest attempt to explain the "why" of God.

In other words, this is my effort to write a challenging book with inadequate ability about an indescribable entity depending almost entirely on the Holy Spirit because I am not capable to complete such a task. In fact, I am most aware of my insufficiency and will need little input from critics of this fact. But the Holy Spirit is sufficient, and so let's give Him credit for what He does despite my shortcomings. The most important resource for this manuscript is the Old and New Testaments of the Protestant Bible. Yes, prayer, meditation, the wisdom of Godly people, and whatever resources, methods, or influences the Holy Spirit chose to use have also assisted in this version you are reading.

Some would call the following fiction; part one.

Before, when there was no matter, substance, or texture, the eternal existed; spirit without limits or boundary, intelligence without measure, power unequaled and unfathomable, wisdom so deep, and knowledge so vast as to only be contained by the eternal. "Contained" or maybe "availed" is a better method of expressing what cannot be seen. In no way is this totally accurate, but it may be a step in the right way of thinking. The eternal one has no limits, such as time, space, walls, or barriers, except those self-imposed.

In the next few pages, an attempt will be made to make more sense of this entity. Yet remember that, as humans, we will always be challenged to understand anything so different from our experiences and concepts. Take heart. You are not the only one nor the last. It is doubtful that anyone will ever understand the eternal until the eternal makes Himself fully known, in all the completeness of existence. Meet God and be amazed.

Buckle up.

Chapter One

An Introduction

Several years ago, a truth came to me and would not leave. The world is, was, and will always be in a flux of change. From the time Paw Paw Jim went to WW1, the war to end all wars, until WW2, there were many changes. Assembly-line production pioneered in the generation before the war, became the new way to mass produce transportation cheaper and making automobiles more available to the general public. Aircraft became safer and were utilized in ways unheard of in 1903. Farming, industry, housing were all affected by the more rural and widespread availability of electricity.

Between WW2 and the '60s, every area of life continued to change. For the most part, these changes enabled people to have more leisure time and a better standard of living, although not every country on the globe benefited. Some governments held back progress, restrained education of the masses, used their resources in selfish living, and were left far behind in these overall advances.

Not all change benefits mankind. As scientist discovered more of God's mysteries, physics, chemistry, biology, astronomy, and engineering, the more in vogue it became to deny God as the Creator. Now theories are taught as unchallengeable tenets of truth. Most, but not all, evolutional theory teachings are made to sound as if they are fact, yet few can be proven by the scientific method, a standard they often require of others. Creation scientists are ridiculed and often left out of the research application process for grants and funding. Not all change benefits mankind.

Since the '60s until present day, the rate of change in American society continues to increase. Lifelong learning will keep people employed as new skills and abilities are constantly required to be valuable to an employer. The person who refuses educational opportunities falls further behind than their more open-minded friends. Vocational skill and hands-on trades are often the middle class's way to compete and surpass college-educated individuals in income and prestige.

Coming from a farm/ranch childhood, people knew where their food originated and how it was processed. Now many people have no idea of the process from field/pasture to table. (Many are grossed out when they discover that process.) No longer does forty to eighty acres provide for a family's income needs. With increased cost of machinery, land, and labor, it is uncommon to find a row crop farm of less than one thousand acres. Many farms and ranches are corporate entities covering many thousands of acres and employing many people. On the other hand, modern farms feed hundreds and thousands of people each, where the old family farm could not. The USA ships food all over the globe to foreign markets, often improving or saving lives.

One other area that has been affected by the swift and ever-more pervasive pace of change is elementary education. The children of this era are not taught the most important lessons of the past, present, and future. Children have been forced, through no fault of their own, to miss out on the love of God. It seems as if today's educational leaders have persistently gerrymandered reasons to filter God out of education while presenting evolution as normal or natural. Educational standards are often written and imposed by people who have little knowledge of God and believe only the ignorant and weak need to believe in the invisible God. Not all change is good.

Because of these reasons and the influx of people who worship other gods or religions, it has become easier to ignore Christianity's major role in the development of our country. The Constitution, Bill of Rights, and heritage of educating our children to know God have been eroded to the point where more and more people are ignorant of a loving Heavenly Father willing to save them from eternal death. Whether they accept Him as their father or reject Him and His teachings is not the point. The impact is they have lost the opportunity to hear and know there is more than unprovable theories to explain life.

This book is an attempt at teaching individuals about this God, the God of the universe, the God of creation, the Holy One. God, who, in three parts, Father, Son, and, Holy Spirit, have shown us love by giving us life. This life is ours to live, under our own conditions, accepting the consequences of freewill. God's love for us is seen daily with gravity, sunshine and rain, food, companionship, and love as well as the intellect and wisdom to build, negotiate, communicate, and form relationships, the memory to avoid second mistakes, identify danger, and protect ourselves. But most importantly, God has taught us right from wrong and given us the choice of which path to follow each and every moment. God desires that we would love Him, and Him alone, more than anyone or anything else. He defines love as obedience and loving others in return. As Bob Goff would say, "Love does." God looks at our intent and our actions and judges righteously. But it is our choice. To love, ignore, or trivialize God is up to each person as an individual decision. But in physical life as well as spiritual life, there are consequences for every choice. Choose wisely.

This book is not

- A comprehensive study of all there is to God.
- Written by a Greek or Hebrew scholar.
- Intended for theologians to debate and critique.
- Perfect, as the writer is human and is known to err (mostly with good intentions).
- The last word on God, Jesus, or the Holy Spirit.
- The Bible.
- A substitute for the Bible.
- An addition or subtraction from God's word.

This book is

- Intended for those who do not know God.
- For those who have yet to meet Jesus.
- For those without the seal of the Holy Spirit.
- To enlighten people on how to live at peace with nearly everyone.
- For those who want to be a part of the big picture.
- For those who seek a spiritual life beyond their time on earth.
- For those who want forgiveness and guilt removed.
- For those who know mankind is not the highest form of life, intellect, or power.
- An opportunity to meet the God of scripture, the Holy Bible.

As stated, this book is to assist the person previously unsure or unaware of the nature of the Trinity. It is a primer, in that every effort was made to use common language and expressions to explain the holy, righteous, perfect, and all-powerful God of the universe. Read and use it to your benefit. May you be blessed by the content and the changes that come your way as you learn about the "Potter" and yourself, the "clay". This is another opportunity to meet God.

Peace be with you all.

Chapter Two

God

Father God Is Holy

God is Holy. The usual terms for holy are "set apart," "sacred," "pure," "unique," or "sanctified." God's holiness goes much beyond these words. He is one of a kind, rarer than rare, as He is *the only God*. (We will get into Trinity later.)

It says in Revelation 4:8, "And the four living creatures, each of them with six wings, are full of eyes all around and within, and day and night they never cease to say, 'Holy, holy, holy, is the Lord God Almighty, who was and is and is to come!'"

In heaven, there are four celestial beings (seraphim) whose special worship is to sing "Holy, Holy, Holy" to God, 24/7, eternally. Why? Because He is! God's holiness is not just a characteristic or trait; it is His identity. God is so set apart from all creation (space, angels and heavenly host, us, everything) that the best comparison that comes to mind would be light versus dark, the brightest light possible contrasted against the darkest dark. And that still does not do the Holy One justice.

His holiness gives Him sovereignty (not to be held accountable by anyone or anything else) over everything. We consider most governments to be sovereign. So consider for a moment how much more is God's sovereignty. God establishes and overturns governments.

Because of His holiness, only He can establish morality. Right, wrong, good, and bad are all His within His domain. If He decides shedding innocent blood is wrong but the death penalty is justified, it is! On the other hand, when God hardens the pharaoh's heart (Exodus 7) yet allows us freewill, it is righteous as He is showing the world His power and sovereignty over mankind. We are not the ones who decide innocence and guilt, except as delegated by Him. He allows governments to make these decisions but not individuals.

Try this as a simple way to accept His holiness. Consider Him whole, complete, absolutely sufficient in and of Himself without any needs to be fulfilled. Everything in creation has needs except God. He is whole. *He is Holy.*

His holiness makes Him so pure, righteous, and beyond reproach; it is blasphemy to misuse His name, worship anything else, or arrogantly compare our righteousness to Him. One of the points I hope atheists will consider in an objective reading of these pages is that God is not threatened by questions of His existence. This inquisitiveness is from Him. No, He wants you to find Him by all the evidence He left for our consideration. The "Word," the order of the universe, the blessings and gifts given by him are undeniable to the honest seeker. It only requires an open mind to accept truth, objective observation, and the desire to seek one's true place in the universe. Once folks accept that no cosmic accident could possibly result in our world, the freedom to find the "Creator" becomes available.

For the agnostic, finding Yahweh requires study and comparison to other supposed deities. Do they truly meet the standard of living and creating life? Are they man-made such as a statue or idol? Yahweh is a man-maker. Do little "g" gods want relationship with you? Yahweh does. Are they holy and righteous? Yahweh is. Do they make and fulfill all promises without fail? Yahweh does. This list could continue an exceptionally long time. But there's no need for it as everyone can see the writing on the wall. What good is believing there is "something out there" if you do not know what it is or your responsibility to it?

God is Holy. As such, there is nothing anywhere to compare Him to; no one else to worship, praise, glorify, emulate, or obey. We all want the answers to our most important questions. Father God is or has those answers because He is the great "I AM."

God is holy.

GOD'S NAME

"I AM" (YAHWEH or YHWH)

God is called by many names or titles in scripture: Adoni, El, El-Elyon, El-Shaddai, and Jehovah Jireh to name a few. These are not His personal names. It is appropriate to use them as they often describe what He has done or will do.

In Exodus 3:13-15, it tells us, "Then Moses said to God, 'If I come to the people of Israel and say to them, "The God of your fathers has sent me to you," and they ask me, "What is his name?" what shall I say to them?' God said to Moses, 'I Am who I Am.' And he said, 'Say this to the people of Israel: "I Am has sent me to you."' God also said to Moses, 'Say this to the people of Israel: "The Lord, the God of your fathers, the God of Abraham, the God of Isaac, and the God of Jacob, has sent me to you." This is my name forever, and thus I Am to be remembered throughout all generations.'"

As with most things about God, even His name is multidimensional. In Exodus 3, Moses meets and converses with Yahweh at a burning bush. This is the first time in recorded history that God choses to reveal His personal name and one major attribute of self, the essence being that He was, He is, and He will be. God is eternal. God exists, is everywhere, is all the time as time does not and cannot contain "I Am." Other ways of saying "I Am" include "the existent one" or "the eternal one." By the way, "eternal," as used in scripture, is not just about future but includes past or whatever was before.

Take a breath, mull this over, and let it simmer. When people grasp this truth, many things must change in their worldview, personal logic, and foundational paradigms. As "I Am," with no beginning or end, God is the only witness to everything that has, is, or will ever happen. There was nothing before Him. There will be nothing after Him. He is "I Am,"

Ready for this? Before Yahweh (our current belief of his name in Hebrew), there was nothing else, there was only Him; no physical matter, intellect, fuel, energy, emotion, nothing. No black holes, stars, quasars, gases, or anything else to use as a catalyst for a big bang or a little pop. God and nothing else exist, until He decided to make the celestial beings as the hosts of heaven. Time has no meaning until Genesis 1, when God decided to create what is this universe.

God Is All-Powerful

Most children (3-103 years old) love superheroes: Superman, Wonder Woman, The X-men, The Avengers, and the list continues. This is not a recent phenomenon. Think Hector, Achilles, Beowulf, Robin Hood, and Tarzan have thrilled readers for many years. The idea of having super strength or uncanny powers helps many compensate for feelings of inadequacy, fear, loss of control, or anxiety brought on by life. They also provide a temporary escape from _____ (you decide).

These are not God. God has no need to compensate for anything. He is all-powerful. When He speaks, creation begins. Stars are arranged into galaxies. At the sound of his voice, universes form, and life happens. God's power creates light, substance, spirit, and time where none was before. Unlike ours, there are no limits to His power. Whatever He wills becomes, and whatever He deletes is gone, at whatever speed He wishes.

God's power cannot be measured. His strength is beyond imagination. He has total control of all He wishes. Many people and even Satan have challenged His authority, but none have prevailed. His commands are obeyed, or consequences occur.

Jesus, in Matthew 19:26, referring to the difference between God and man, said, "With man this is impossible, but with God all things are possible". The context had to do with, how can the rich get into Heaven. But Jesus could have used any number of examples and the statement would still be true. Realize this: God can and does, whatever He wills, because He has limitless power.

God is all-powerful.

GOD IS EVERYWHERE

The fancy word is "omnipresent." God is Spirit, and as Spirit, He is not bound by time, space, or matter. Hence, His essence is everywhere all the time. Remember, earlier, the words about His name and holiness. Part of "I was, I Am, I will be" is because He is Spirit. He exists in what happened before, what is happening now, and what will happen in the future.

Being "set apart" is also seen in that God's awareness is wherever He wills, regardless. Being Spirit makes His natural form invisible to our eyes. Granted there are times when He takes on human form, but this is not His eternal essence (Genesis 18). This invisibility has historically been a troublesome issue to many people in that they like to see what they worship, curse, or oddly enough, ignore. Voila, they create idols, invent gods of their liking or imagination, or worship the creation (wealth, power, etc.) instead of the Creator. But this is a human shortcoming.

God, being Spirit, can be everywhere all the time, making Him available to us in any circumstance. Examples include providing comfort to the divorced parent, the depressed, and betrayed, challenging one soul to make the right choice and available to forgive those who repent. As Spirit, there is nothing He cannot see, hear, know, address, or allow as it suits His plans.

1 Peter 4:6: "For this is why the gospel was preached even to those who are dead, that though judged in the flesh the way people are, they might live in the spirit the way God does."

God is everywhere.

GOD IS ALL-KNOWING

God knows everything—everything! He knows math, science, languages, thoughts, wisdom, psychology, universe, galaxy, quasars, black holes, the secrets of who, how, what, where, when, and why of *everything*. There is a quip often repeated about "people who think they know everything annoy those of us who really do." Well, God could have authored that phrase, and it would be true.

People are so arrogant in their ignorance and annoying in their futile quest to prove something God said was untrue. The scientist who publishes truth circa 1450 CE is rebuked and ridiculed by the scientist who publishes truth in 1850, and on it goes. A doctor's cutting-edge procedure is later debunked as being equal to bloodletting in the 1700s to cure pneumonia. The only truth that is never proved inaccurate is God's! What He states is truth. (By the way, be careful with believing there is "your truth." You have beliefs, opinions, and experiences. You may use them as a guide. But if it is the "truth," it is from God and will not change with time, circumstance, or the next PC phrase.)

Doesn't it make perfect sense that the author of life would know more about it than the one who is a product of God's gift? To explain in detail why and how God knowledge exists is beyond human ability. To see it is simple. The earth rotates, fish swim, gravity keeps us from flying into space, nature abhors a vacuum, and light overcomes darkness. Some would say "it's natural or evolution," and they would be wrong unless they accept that God uses limited evolution and makes things look so simple that it seems natural. God knows *everything*, we don't, and on earth, we never will. Accept it, but do not despair, He tells us all we need to know and much more.

If you really want to have knowledge and wisdom, read His word, especially the Psalms, Proverbs, Job, and Ecclesiastes. There is wisdom of some nature throughout the Bible, but it is quite easy to find in these above mentioned books.

God is all-knowing.

GOD IS CREATOR

Genesis 1:1-5: "In the beginning, God created the heavens and the earth. The earth was without form and void, and darkness was over the face of the deep. And the Spirit of God was hovering over the face of the waters. And God said, 'Let there be light,' and there was light. And God saw that the light was good. And God separated the light from the darkness. God called the light Day, and the darkness he called Night. And there was evening and there was morning, the first day."

As to Creator, let's begin by looking at the word "create" itself. In the Spiritual world, to create is to bring into existence something from nothing. Think about this for a moment.

To create is beyond any human capability. A baby is not created; it is conceived. A skyscraper is built, not created. Atoms are not created; they are discovered and studied. Humans cannot take nonexistence and speak it into existence. God can, and God did. This world and all basic physical properties that have or will be, came from His creation. As a potter takes clay and molds it into a form or container, God willed what is and spoke it into existence. The difference between the potter and God is the potter has to use God's clay as he can never create clay from *nothingness*. God did.

Take a deep breath and consider for a moment the intellect and power involved to create our universe. God spoke into being water, earth, minerals, plant life, fish, animals, gravity, light, DNA, chromosomes, stars, and the list goes on and on. For a Spirit to speak matter into existence in so many forms and conditions, placed exactly the right distance from a star, you get the point—He is a Creator par excellent.

God is Creator.

Connecting Dots and Thoughts

"And now a few words about our sponsor . . ." As a child, this phrase usually meant a commercial was coming. That was my signal to grab a snack, go to the privy, or if close enough, to aggravate my siblings before the TV show returned. The sponsor, in that case, wanted to sell me something, and as a farm boy, I had little money to spend, limited transportation, and no need of Geritol, a Timex, or a Buick. I pray I am more mature now than I was then when it comes to God. The pause inserted here is to help focus some thoughts and verbiage from the previous pages.

God exists as His name implies, always has, does, and always will. As a Spirit with unlimited power, strength, and knowledge, He is able to be present everywhere, always, and at once. This is just another part of His holiness as nothing, no one, nada, and zilch, is able to do or be God. As such, He, and only He, could be the Creator. As Creator, He becomes LORD of all that is created. He is master of the universe, king of the world, owner, landlord, and boss. As much as it pains people everywhere to have to accept that mankind is not God, it galls them even more that there is one who is and has the right to act as such. Why? Well, among other things, God gets to make the rules, assign morality, and reward or punish those who defy His words. When it comes to God's laws, coloring outside the lines is never encouraged and most often punished. Please think about this and reflect deeply. You have just read a truth.

Oh, go ahead and grab a snack before turning the page. The commercial is over.

Some Would Call This Fiction

Something just happened. No, not over 60 billion years, 48 billion, 24 billion, 18 billion, 11 billion years, or any other decreasing number of billions of years. Something happened in an organized, sequential, logical, and perfect order. God spoke, and history began. The eternal, revealed as God, spoke something into existence that never existed before. Creation, matter, liquid, chemicals, the whole periodic table came into being and took the form, function, and activity intended by the all-knowing and all-powerful God.

From darkness to light was only four words: "Let there be light." The implications are stupendous. Darkness, where nothing grows, is overcome by light. Light is where communication is illuminated, options become unlimited; growth unrestrained is now possible, no, more than possible, they become mandatory.

Where darkness is found, it is only because God allows it to be. When God said those four words, He immediately interjected Himself and His influence into creation. God is light as John the apostle and friend Jesus explains in 1 John 1.

1 John 1:5: "This is the message we have heard from him and proclaim to you, that God is light, and in him is no darkness at all."

Chew on that for a while. The light from the sun, moon, and stars is among the fourth part of creation. God brought Himself into the creation before He spoke the celestial elements into being.

Fiction? You decide ….. after you read the book.

QUALITIES AND CHARACTERISTICS

Truth/Honesty

One of the things that brings followers comfort is that God does not lie. God takes honesty to an unbelievable (for most people) level. What is remarkable about this quality is, it is self-imposed. God could lie if He would allow Himself, but that is totally inconsistent with who and what He is. He has chosen never to lie, and so it is and will remain. "God is the same yesterday, today, and forever" (Hebrews 13:8).

He is blunt in his honesty, seldom breaking things to people "gently." Truth is truth, and He doesn't candy-coat the message. Most often it is in a "matter of fact" manner that He shares truth, but regardless of process, the content is accurate, true, reliable, and dependable. On two occasions, Moses asked God to help bring water for the people of Israel. In Exodus 17, God tells Moses to strike a rock and water flowed from it. In Numbers 20, a similar situation occurred, but Moses took credit for God's miracle and also struck a rock He was supposed to speak to. God's response is recorded in the next passage. Numbers 20: 12: "And the Lord said to Moses and Aaron, 'Because you did not believe in me, to uphold me as holy in the eyes of the people of Israel, therefore you shall not bring this assembly into the land that I have given them." Because of Moses's ill-advised behavior, God very matter-of-factly told his servant, "You will not enter the promised land."

He may choose to tell a message in portions, but it is not to mislead. Rather, He often reveals Himself or an event in partial prophesies, in part, so (1) man will realize he is dependent on God for information, and (2) as the event unfolds, we can see His glory in the fulfillment. He also is so deep in knowledge of things in which we have no knowledge at all, that to reveal even a part would distract us from the important messages of life and death. Other times He condenses a story (creation) because it is less about "how" and more about "why" (us) He created the cosmos.

Now back to the comfort followers experience with an honest Holy God. No tricks, no broken promises, no double dealing, and most of all, no disappointments are found in Him. Some folks will object to this last statement. Read it again. If we are ever disappointed in God, it is not in His truth but in our desire for a different non-God promised outcome. In other words, we may assign something to God that He never said He would do and then become disappointed that we were unable to pull His strings. Sorry, but that would not be God but rather a fantasy of who we want God to be. Childish, are we not? What God says will happen will happen. What he says He will do, He will do. What He curses is cursed, and who he blesses is blessed. He is faithful to His word, Himself, and His creation.

As stated in scripture, Numbers 23:19, "God is not a man, that He should lie, Nor a son of man, that He should repent; Has He said, and will He not do it? Or has He spoken, and will He not make it good?"

And you can take that to the bank!

Truth/Honesty are inherent with God.

God Is Love

1 John 4:8: "Anyone who does not love does not know God, because God is love."

Love is behavior. Love is action. Love is often visible, has impact, and consequence. When God says He loves us, He is not referring to a fleeting feeling of fondness, attraction, or lust. His love is shown by what He does. He created a perfect world, designed our bodies in His likeness and image, gave us paradise, and when we sinned, He had a backup plan in place. Plan B involved an unbelievable sacrifice on the part of God the Father as well as God the Son. (More on this in the next section.) The point is that when God says He is love, we are hearing something much larger, deeper, and more impactful than an emotional reference with no substance.

His love is seen in a creation that perfectly meets our physical needs. Consider our atmosphere with the perfect balance of oxygen and other gasses, a sun placed just close enough to provide warmth, growing seasons and rest, and a gravity that keeps us from hurtling to outer space and safely planted on the ground. His love is seen in our need for fellowship in all its various forms, from family to friends, social groups, community, as well as to the spiritual aspect when we worship, commune, and commit ourselves to Him as He does to His followers.

His love is seen in our freewill and our power of choice. He would revel (Party in Heaven) if we all chose to make Him the center of our being, but He respects the fact that it isn't love, if it is done by coercion. He respects our choice even when it is in our worst interest. We can reject Him, His plans, His promises, and everything else, but it is a really bad decision, and He hopes we will reconsider. God knows love also requires letting go, even when it hurts Him.

*Special note: The fact that God is love, is truth. Also He is also more than one-dimensional. Please do not mistake this truth to mean He will always do what you want, think, or that His love trumps His desire for obedience and justice. As many have said, God's desire for obedience and justice is evidence of His love. This is due to the fact that He knows better how we need to live than we do. He is the author of life."

God is love.

JUST/JUSTICE

Romans 12:14-21: "Bless those who persecute you; bless and do not curse them. Rejoice with those who rejoice, weep with those who weep. Live in harmony with one another. Do not be haughty, but associate with the lowly. Never be wise in your own sight. Repay no one evil for evil, but give thought to do what is honorable in the sight of all. If possible, so far as it depends on you, live peaceably with all. Beloved, never avenge yourselves, but leave it to the wrath of God, for it is written, 'Vengeance is mine, I will repay, says the Lord.' To the contrary, 'if your enemy is hungry, feed him; if he is thirsty, give him something to drink; for by so doing you will heap burning coals on his head.' Do not be overcome by evil, but overcome evil with good."

The previous scriptures was written by the apostle Paul to the Christians in Rome some two thousand years ago. Then as now, people were being hurt and wanted relief. Paul advised them in the way of Jesus by saying, try to get along with others, and in the end, God will provide justice.

God is balanced. He demonstrates love and blesses, yet He also is just and punishes. Since God allows freewill, He also has to allow evil to exist among the righteous. That does not mean He condones it or quits loving us. Look at that last sentence again! It does mean that bad will happen to bad and good alike because it is the nature of man to sin against God and that often affects us. When we hear the masses ask, "How can a loving God allow murder, rape, _____ (fill in the blank)?" you are hearing either someone who doesn't know God or someone in pain looking for answers. For those in pain, this statement is of little comfort. It is still true. Man is the sinner, not God. He has to allow freewill, so we can choose to love and serve Him or do as we please.

God is just. For example, He punishes those who sin, whether by character assassination (gossip) or a political assassination (murder). Both are sins against a Holy God (all sin is against God) with ramifications in the world. The problem for many of us is we want justice for others and mercy for ourselves. A second issue is we want justice/revenge now, not later.

God provides justice in many forms. Natural consequences exist as well as the military, courts, and other governmental entities. He also uses one nation to punish another (war) when it suits His will. You can see many examples of this in the Old Testament. There is one time period set aside to finalize justice and punish the evil of this world. In scripture, it is simply referred to as Judgment Day, the day set aside for God to review the lives of all people who have not become a part of Jesus's church. (More on this later.) Those people will be held accountable for their sin, evil, hurting, misbehavior, and sentenced to hell for punishment.

This is just! Why? Because the Creator makes the rules and sets the consequences for everyone. The Holy One made provision for all to come live with Him (Heaven) but allows for us to choose to do as we please. What he does not allow, is for us to pick the consequence for our behavior. He does that.

Yes, Virginia, there is justice. There is a just God. He will exact vengeance against sinners. It just ticks us off that He does not do it when and how we want it to occur. We want quick justice when we are hurt, but we want mercy when we hurt others. We judge others by impact but want ourselves to be judged by intent. God exists above the fray and judges by righteous judgment.

Remember, we choose how we act, but a just God determines the consequences. Enough said for now.

God is just and will provide justice.

God Observes and Is Aware

Jeremiah 23:24: "'Can a man hide himself in hiding places, So I do not see him?' declares the LORD 'Do I not fill the heavens and the earth?' declares the LORD."

God sees everything. There is nothing that goes on, above or under the soil, that happens outside of His awareness. He observes our thoughts, feelings, behaviors, and outcomes. He knows when a bird dies and when a puppy is born. Wind currents, cloud patterns, light spectrums, and humidity changes may bring about jobs for meteorologists, but they are no big deal to Him. Change is a constant, and God is the author of change. No one can remain the same in the presence of God, and He often is the catalyst of what He later observes. God is in the moment as well as in the beginning and the end. In the moment, He remains aware as to be available to those who seek Him and to observe those who do not. His observation allows for Him to comfort those who request, and His awareness makes the depth of our need crystal clear. This trait is made possible by His being a Spirit that has no boundaries or constraints. It also proceeds out of His love for us and His desire to be the core of our lives. He knows all about us and wishes us to know all about Him. He sees us as we are and as we ought to be. He knows what we respond to and what pains still haunt us. We are never alone even in the depths of depression or the heights of personal achievement. He sees it all.

There are no secret sins. Oh, we make great efforts to hide them from public view, yet we cannot hide them from God. He is observant, He knows our sins, yet that does not necessarily require Him to act in a preordained manner. He can act, wait, forgive, or allow us to learn from the natural or imposed consequence.

The great advantage of an aware and observant God is His followers know He is available. We can ask for help, forgiveness, or the courage and strength to change. We also know that we do not have to make excuses or explain our thinking because He knows, so we can skip all that and go straight to the source of life for whatever we need. There are no secrets from God.

God observes and is aware.

God Is Faithful

There are many passages in scripture about God's faithfulness. The following is one of my favorites: 1 John 1:9-10: "If we confess our sins, he is faithful and just to forgive us our sins and to cleanse us from all unrighteousness. If we say we have not sinned, we make him a liar, and his word is not in us."

So what does this mean? Faithful is much like the idea of being dependable but much larger. There is a surety, firmness, or constancy to God, especially regarding His promises. God is faithful in so many ways. He is faithful to His people. He is faithful to His promises. He is faithful to His covenant. He is faithful to His word.

In the Old Testament, God levied consequences against Adam, Eve, and Satan (Genesis 3). Man would work, and it would be a struggle. Childbirth pain would increase, yet women would desire her man. Satan would be the lowest of the low, striking at our heel only to have his head crushed. All three continue. In the Old Testament, God made a promise to Noah that we no longer need fear a worldwide flood. God blessed Israel if they were faithful to Him, yet He allowed them to repent and return to Him after many departures. Why? He told them they would break the covenant and that He would forgive if they repented (Leviticus 26).

There are too many examples to list, but the truth of God is that He is unchanging and that He does not lie. That makes him faithful. There is none so faithful as God, and He expects His people to adopt this characteristic. To an atheist, this will not matter until Judgment Day. To Christians, this is very comforting. To the rest of mankind, please consider the impact His faithfulness will have on you.

1 Corinthians 10: 13: "No temptation has overtaken you that is not common to man. God is faithful, and he will not let you be tempted beyond your ability, but with the temptation he will also provide the way of escape, that you may be able to endure it."

God is faithful.

GOD PROVIDES

The "I pulled myself up by my own bootstraps" people ought to pause and see how much of their success comes from God. Yes, most of us work hard for success. That does not mean we did it on our own. Paul tells Timothy in scripture that it is unwise to think they did it "my way."

1 Timothy 6:17 "As for the rich in this present age, charge them not to be haughty, nor to set their hopes on the uncertainty of riches, but on God, who richly provides us with everything to enjoy."

Father God is the great provider, no, not in a Santa Clause way, rather in a very practical way. In varying degrees, we all receive light, air, water, sustenance, a very fruitful planet, physical abilities, and intellect. The planet came ready for human habitation, exactly close enough to and yet far away from the sun for our existence. Water is in abundance. Soil and crust are able to filter water and return it to drinkable quality unless tampered with. We are hardwired to a herd mentality, communication ability, complementarity, and emotions. These he offers too all.

On a more individual basis, He often provides special requests for those who commune with Him in prayer and obedience (which God sees as love). Most often it is His followers who receive these provisions, but on occasion, He does this for those He calls, in hopes that they will respond to the love He has for all. In the Old Testament, He returned the life of a son to his mother (1 Kings 17:17-24). She had shown kindness to a prophet of God, and He provided what she wanted most. He also cured the leprosy of a non-Israelite military commander (2 Kings 5:1-14). At the time of these events, Israel was suffering from their sin, and God was not treating them as before, in hopes of their repentance.

The most special provisions that God offers are spiritual. He calls us to know Him. He provides weapons to fight spiritual battles. His word, truth, salvation, prayer, and the Holy Spirit are to guide us, and the list goes on. In our weakness, He provides help with avoiding or resisting temptation. He even provides the words we need when defending His truth to unbelievers.

God provides.

GOD BLESSES

No, I didn't sneeze. In fact, nowadays, you rarely hear "God bless you" after a sneeze. "Bless you" (left out "God"), "Gesundheit," "wear a mask," or "cover your mouth" are the most common responses. But God does bless His children. This is above and beyond being a provider. As inferred, as a provider, most of God's provisions are for all. But the blessings I refer to now are more personal and individualized.

God has provided many blessings to me, my family, and my friends. Doors have been opened, opportunities offered, financial needs met, health request beyond what medicine could provide. In fact, one of the marks of God's special provisions is that they almost always occur when there can be no other explanation. A friend of mine used the phrase "the just-in-time God." Over and over, when nearly all hope is extinguished, the provision arrives, and there is no other plausible reason but God.

Some will try to explain this by coincidence, serendipity, or accident. People who deny God must rationalize or make up something in explanation. Words are cheap, but movement and events speak much more convincingly. An elderly pastor friend, now retired, used a local expression, "Talk is cheap, but whiskey cost money."

When you ask true believers to share a story of how God answered a prayer with a special blessing, their eyes show excitement. They often will go into detail on how, where, and when; they were desperate and called out in prayer and in a clear, unmistakable manner, God blessed them. Many times God blesses in ways that astound or surprise the believer.

Other times God blesses those who do His will without them praying for assistance. A great example is told in scripture about Solomon early in his reign. God tells him to ask for any gift, and Solomon asks for wisdom to rule over Israel. God grants this and then adds riches, honor, etc., because Solomon was not greedy in his request (1 Kings 3:1-15). God blesses those He loves.

Proverbs 3:33 "The Lord's curse is on the house of the wicked, but he blesses the dwelling of the righteous."

God blesses.

GOD DISCIPLINES

Now let us make clear that the word "discipline," as used in scripture, can mean punish or teach. It never means temptation to sin. That comes from within our lusts and desires for those things we do not need. It is also influenced by Satan, the father of all lies. God does not tempt mankind to sin, but He allows trials in our lives so we can grow in knowledge of our dependence on Him. He also uses these tests to teach spiritual truths and help us grow in the fruits of the Spirit.

Galatians 5:22-23: "But the fruit of the Spirit is love, joy, peace, patience, kindness, goodness, faithfulness, gentleness, self-control; against such things there is no law."

Consider a moral struggle you finally handled correctly. Then look at the list above and pick out the fruit you received by following God's will instead of the wrong choice. When you think of God as a loving father (He is), it makes sense how a parent, who genuinely loves, will discipline rather than spoil or ignore a misbehaving child. In fact, that is often how we act. We covet other's stuff and often steal, whine, or misbehave to get ours. How many marriages have been destroyed by selfish use of money by one partner? Control becomes dominance, fondness becomes lust, celebration becomes drunkenness, stories become false witness, and justice becomes revenge.

God knew, from the beginning, that there was a great need for restraint and boundaries. People push and ignore social and legal boundaries, so civil and criminal law had to be imposed. God loves justice and true scales but hates a biased judge or those who take a bribe.

Deuteronomy 8:5 "Know then in your heart that, as a man disciplines his son, the Lord your God disciplines you."

Yes even the human Jesus had to learn as we do. That said, I suspect the lessons He learned early in life made it possible to endure the cross.

Hebrews 5:7-10: "In the days of his flesh, Jesus offered up prayers and supplications, with loud cries and tears, to him who was able to save him from death, and he was heard because of his reverence. Although he was a son, he learned obedience through what he suffered. And being made perfect, he became the source of eternal salvation to all who obey him, being designated by God a high priest after the order of Melchizedek."

God disciplines.

GOD FORGIVES

Thrilled, happy, ye-haw. Why? Because God forgives. Why? Because we all need forgiveness. Why? Because we all sin. Why? Because we (pick one or more) covet, lie, steal, fornicate, rape, kill, assault, insult, blaspheme, curse, rage, riot, engage in gluttony, gossip, drunkenness, and the list goes on. Human beings start out so pure and become so filthy by sin that they can only be reconciled to God by forgiveness. Gracefully, God does forgive sin.

I'll let you in on a little-known secret. *All* sin is against God. No, I did not stutter. *All* sin is against God. God is the moral authority for the universe, and it is His laws that we break. Yes, I know you and I, have been hurt many times by the sins of others and have hurt self and others with our behavior. That does not change the fact that the sin is against God. He is the lawgiver, holy and righteous. As such, He is the offended party when we (His creation) break His law or moral codes.

Fortunately, He knows us and our tendency to sin better than we do and has offered His children a way to gain forgiveness. Once we experience Godly sorrow for the sin, we ask for forgiveness. Then, when He perceives sincerity in our regret and request, He forgives. Pretty simple, huh? What is even more cool, in my opinion, is, it is as if, it never happened. He says He "remembers it no more." He has no gunny sack where He stores it and brings it up later to shame us or hold it against us.

But someone is saying "when Joe hit me," that was a sin against me. Well, yes, you were hit, hurt, and offended. But without the moral code and laws of God, who is to say that Joe "can't" hit you? …. You? What gives you the power to tell Joe what he can or cannot do? Society? They could just as easily say it is open season on you. God's laws, rules, and ordinances are universal. Exceptions to the rule are just that—exceptions. And exceptions do not change the rule.

Does Joe owe you an apology? Probably. Do you need to forgive him? Yes! Will you do it? Think about this: God is represented in Matthew 6:7-15 as forgiving, forgiving us in the same manner we forgive others. So it befits us in this respect that if we wish to have forgiveness, we have to offer it to those who offend us. God takes His cue from us on how to forgive us. He will judge and forgive us as we have done so to others. The idea is "keep the bar low" for your own sake. Try to forgive as quickly and sincerely as possible.

Please accept the difference between forgive and forget. Forgiving others is required. This is essential. But God does not demand you to forget. He gave us memory as a self-defense mechanism, among other things (like finding your way home). No, the memory of the offense, pain, or situation can help us avoid future pain. A little-known secret is that often we *can* forget. It may take time and a sincere change in relationship, but I have experienced this phenomenon many times.

Please do not think this is all we have to say about forgiveness. When the topic is salvation (last chapter), there will be more to say about forgiveness. The following scripture gives me great comfort. I hope it does the same for you.

Psalm 103:10-12: "He does not deal with us according to our sins, nor repay us according to our iniquities. For as high as the heavens are above the earth, so great is his steadfast love toward those who fear him; as far as the east is from the west, so far does he remove our transgressions from us."

God forgives.

GOD IS PATIENT

Numbers 14:18: "The LORD is slow to anger and abundant in loving-kindness, forgiving iniquity and transgression; but He will by no means clear the guilty, visiting the iniquity of the fathers on the children to the third and the fourth generations."

Yahweh is patient overall with humans. Yes, there are individual circumstances where He acted swiftly. Nadab and Abihu (Leviticus 10), Ananias and Sapphira (Acts 5), as well as Uzza (2 Samuel 6), might have an argument over this statement, but Uzza broke a specific command that he, as a priest, knew perfectly. Nadab and Abihu had God's recipe for incense yet used their own. Ananias and Sapphira lied to the Holy Spirit while trying to seek honor for their behavior. All knew better. God, in His glory, made a point to the world that you do not break His rules on holiness without consequence. Note that all three situations are exceptions to the rule of God's long-suffering, but that does not negate His almost constant patience.

Regardless of these and some other incidents, God is patient and long-suffering in His waiting for us to seek and obey Him. Remember, "exceptions to the rule do not change the rule. They are simply exceptions." God waits a hundred years before the flood (Genesis 6), generations before the united kingdom of David became the divided, conquered, and dispersed Jews of the Old Testament. He has waited nearly two thousand years since Jesus's ascension to heaven.

Although He waits patiently for people to choose Him or eternal death, no one has a guarantee of tomorrow. So even though He is more patient than many (all) of us deserve, there is an end to his long-suffering with everyone. In fact, if you set the standard for how tolerant God should be, most, if not all, of us would be dead. There are many among us who can't handle the daily commute without wishing death to many around us. God endures more than traffic jams and bad drivers.

Why is He so persevering? There are reasons beyond my understanding, but the few I grasp start with He knows us! God knows our frailties, double-mindedness, indecisiveness, emotional tirades, confusion, selfishness, and the list goes on. As our Creator, He gave us "freewill" to accept and obey Him or to reject and rebel against Him. Either choice comes with consequences: eternal life in His presence, rewarded by serving and glorifying Him, or eternal death after a brief time of living as we please. Ask someone over eighty, and most will tell you the years have flashed by. Eternity has no end.

My thought is this: God is long-suffering to give us many opportunities to choose Him as our God. That is good news! What Satan hopes is that we will not choose God. So the evil one says, "Sure, repent and change ….. later. There is plenty of time for you to change later. Don't be in a hurry," snicker, snicker.

Think about it.

2 Peter 3:9: "The Lord is not slow about His promise, as some count slowness, but is patient toward you, not wishing for any to perish but for all to come to repentance.

God is patient.

God Will Punish Sin

Romans 12:19b: "Never take your own revenge, beloved, but leave room for the wrath of God, for it is written, 'VENGEANCE IS MINE, I WILL REPAY,' says the Lord.

Yahweh is holy, and among other things, it means He will make things right. Sin will be punished. When His people are hurt, He will exact justice on the evil, bring vengeance on the unrighteous, and exact retribution on the offender. God does care about His people and wants them to know He will right the wrongs done to them in this life.

When we are hurt, we want to see the vengeance done to them right *now*. Some of us want to gloat and rub salt in the wound, and God rarely does things that way. Consider all the insults and hurts Noah and his seven experienced while building the Ark (Genesis6-8) Do we think he was happy to see his enemies or neighbors, die in the flood? I doubt it. "Noah walked with God" prior to the flood (that is why he and his family were saved), so I believe he was sad to hear the screams of his fellow citizens, pleading to be saved, as they drown. But as a righteous man, he knew God's justice was holy and long overdue.

If you choose to read Genesis 6, you will find that the world had become so full of sin that this is about all they dwelled on daily. Think about that for a moment. Everyone (-8 people) were imagining theft or rape or murder or adultery as they walked down the street. If you had a nice dwelling, someone was scheming on how to get it from you. Child torture, animal abuse, spousal assaults, drunkenness, and elderly cruelty were not occasional occurrences that shock the neighborhood but rather a daily occurrence. We recoil in horror over suicide bombings, as we should, but the evil described in this chapter goes far beyond the level of evil we see today that stuns even the average citizen.

So is it right for God to exact revenge? Yes! It is not only right, but it is also required that a Holy God punish, destroy (you pick the word), an evil world. Some would say, "Well, that is genocide." No, genocide is when one nation seeks to destroy another people out of prejudice or bigotry. "Sinocide" (my term) is when the only moral authority in the universe says "I've been patient long enough" and brings their lives to an end. It is not based on one people judging another people (equals) but on the Creator making the decision that this creation that bears His image is too hard-hearted or vile to redeem and so He saves the only eight who live in harmony with Him.

Shocking to you? Only if you believe you have the right to limit God or dictate to Him right and wrong. Since this writer is one of you also, I know we are too fickle, ignorant, and shallow to consistently determine what only God can justly enable. We lack the capacity on our own to be holy and righteous, and that alone disqualifies us from determining if God should or should not act in any way He pleases. In Psalms 115, God is compared to the man-made idols and false gods of the Old Testament. The one line that should catch your eye is verse 3: "Our God is in the heavens; he does all that he pleases."

When people say someone does as he pleases, they are referring to a "cut-up" or someone "out of control." God is never out of control. He is Yahweh. This is enough said on this topic.

God will punish sin.

God Is Our Confidence

Job 4:6 "Is not your fear of God your confidence, and the integrity of your ways your hope?"

A friend of Job asks this question of his humbled and hurting friend. If you continue through the whole book of Job, the answer is yes. The word "fear," as used here, can also mean awe or respect. When you know you belong to God, there is great confidence in your path, security in times of trouble, and peace when others tremble. In 2 Corinthians 3, scripture tells us the sufficiency we get through God. This assurance is partly because of faith and partly because, as a rule, God protects His own. Christians also try to get along with others as best they are able.

Don't get me wrong, this confidence is not a foolhardy approach to life. Rather, it is a sense that we are on mission, living His way, and He blesses those who love Him. By accepting the proverbs and instruction of the Bible, we avoid sticking our noses in others' business. We give more often than we loan. Enemies are treated with respect and occasionally quit being of concern or, in the best of outcomes, become friends.

I also am not saying we never end up in conflict, pain, or crisis. We do, but there is such a sense of sureness knowing the all-powerful God is in your corner and will never leave you alone. We can rely on the knowledge that no one (Satan, people) can destroy our soul because only God has that power, and He loves His own. Being a child of God can lead to a more stress-free, cool, and confident life if we trust and obey *His* word. Like the old song says, "Trust and obey, for there is no other way, to be happy in Jesus, but to trust and obey."

Romans 12:17-18: "Repay no one evil for evil, but give thought to do what is honorable in the sight of all. If possible, so far as it depends on you, live peaceably with all."

God is our confidence.

God Is the Father of All

John 20:17: "'Don't cling to me,' Jesus told her, 'since I have not yet ascended to the Father. But go to my brothers and tell them that I am ascending to my Father and your Father, to my God and your God.'"

As names go, Jesus reveals Yahweh as "Father" and rocks the whole Jewish community. How dare He call the Creator, the eternal one, all-powerful, ever-present, all-knowing, and the great I Am, Father? It shocks their sense of awe and piety to see or hear God as a Father. That makes Him too approachable. That makes Jesus (who claimed to be His Son) appear to blaspheme and worthy of stoning. What confusion! Father?

But not only does Jesus use this language, He also taught it to others. Before long, all His followers were using the same reference, not in a slang or irreverent way, but as an endearing title of relationship and love. The Old Testament had never presumed to be so "familiar" in addressing God. Granted, in the books Psalms and Micah, God was referred to as Father, but it could easily be misapplied to "David" or Abraham. No, this was too far out to consider. The Pharisees, especially the high priests, found their hackles up and angry thoughts taking over.

But stop, dwell on it. A father plants the seed of existence, provides for growth, works for his offspring, and gives them his name. What better description of Yahweh than as a Father, our Father, the Creator, and sustainer of all mankind.

God is the Father of all.

GOD IS THREE (TRINITY)

John 17:1-5: "When Jesus had spoken these words, he lifted up his eyes to heaven, and said, 'Father, the hour has come; glorify your Son that the Son may glorify you, since you have given him authority over all flesh, to give eternal life to all whom you have given him. And this is eternal life, that they know you, the only true God, and Jesus Christ whom you have sent. I glorified you on earth, having accomplished the work that you gave me to do. And now, Father, glorify me in your own presence with the glory that I had with you before the world existed."

Okay, so I cannot delay this any longer. God is one, and God is three. Strap in and open minds required.

Yahweh is one, Jesus the Messiah is one and the Holy Spirit is one. God is the Triune Deity so completely united in purpose, essence, and being that He is one and He is three in one. It is not an either-or situation but a both-and revelation. God the Father, God the Son, and God the Holy Spirit are one in unity but three in activity. God the Father is a Spirit whose "face" is unseen, except by Jesus and the Holy Spirit. God the Son began in a Spirit form but gave up His rightful place to become human and live among us. The Holy Spirit is God who has dwelled on Earth since the "beginning" (Genesis 1) and is the active miraculous force for God's will and our conduit (prayer interpreter) to the Father. Accepting this truth will often assist in understanding scripture. Many Bible passages make more sense when you know it is Jesus speaking instead of the Father or Holy Spirit.

A friend of mine, Matt Bedell, told me this analogy. He credits his departed mother, Carole Bedell, for teaching him. I was blessed to meet her sometime later while working with the Bread Shed in Poplar Bluff, Mo. She taught Matt that water is water. Water is not more or less water when it is ice. Water is water. Water is still water when it is steam. Water is water. Obviously, water is water when liquid. Yet the water in different forms has different effects, mobility, and appearance. It is still water, and God is God as Father, Son, or Holy Spirit, and He/They are one. Hopefully, that helps. It was an eye-opener for me. I have since heard others use the same explanation, but that day with Matt was my first time to hear and absorb this revelation. I hope it works for you. Let us look at some scripture that will reinforce the Triune God.

Genesis 1:1-2 "In the beginning, God created the heavens and the earth. The earth was without form and void, and darkness was over the face of the deep. And the Spirit of God was hovering over the face of the waters."

In the first verse of the Bible, the word "God," in the original language of Hebrew, is "Elohim," which is plural. The second verse mentions the Holy Spirit, which is a second part of the Triune God. So right out of the gate, we are told God exists in more than one part of self.

John 1:1-3: "In the beginning was the Word, and the Word was with God, and the Word was God. He was in the beginning with God. All things were made through him, and without him was not any thing made that was made."

Again, we see the plurality of God when Jesus, "the word," is there at the beginning of creation.

Isaiah 9:6 "For unto us a Child is born, Unto us a Son is given; And the government will be upon His shoulder. And His name will be called Wonderful, Counselor, Mighty God, Everlasting Father, Prince of Peace."

This prophecy of Jesus by one of Israel's greatest prophets identifies Jesus as "Mighty God, Everlasting Father."

The New Testament makes it much more transparent. I will use a few references, but there are many more if you care to look them up.

Matthew 3:16-17 "And when Jesus was baptized, immediately he went up from the water, and behold, the heavens were opened to him, and he saw the Spirit of God descending like a dove and coming to rest on him; and behold, a voice from heaven said, 'This is my beloved Son, with whom I am well pleased.'"

First, I wish I could have been there. Second, I doubt many, if any, recognized the event for what it was. The eternal invisible God speaks for mankind to hear, while the Holy Spirit, in the form of a dove, lights on Jesus, while Jesus, God in flesh, is being recognized for the who and what He has done or will do on earth, all in one place and one time, discernable by human senses for the first time in history. wow! wow! wow! (There is much more to this passage I will address in other writings (LORD willing) in the future.)

John 14:26 "But the Helper, the Holy Spirit, whom the Father will send in my name, he will teach you all things and bring to your remembrance all that I have said to you."

In this passage, Jesus is preparing His disciples for His return to heaven. But He promises the Holy Spirit will be sent to them by God to help them after Jesus leaves.

One last reference, in 2 Corinthians 13:14, the apostle Paul says, "The grace of the Lord Jesus Christ and the love of God and the fellowship of the Holy Spirit be with you all."

This serves to close a letter to Christians who knew of the Trinity, offering comfort. They are being reminded that all of the Eternal was there in support of their efforts. If you take the time to look, you can learn some of the different roles described/mentioned in these passages.

God is one, and God is Trinity, and there is no discrepancy or error in this statement. YAHWEH is the great "I AM." The unity, power, and purpose of the Triune God is truth. Some would call this fiction.

The eternal, the existent one, the great I Am, Elohim, Jehovah Jireh, and a plethora (fancy, huh?) of other names and identities is bound to tell the truth because He is truth; teaching and demonstrating love because He is love; providing civil, legal, and spiritual justice because in His holiness, He is truly just; completely aware of all that occurs and cognizant of each impact because He is everywhere, observing even the tiniest detail. He never sleeps or daydreams.

So faithful, He can always be depended upon to do as He says, keep His promises, and is our confidence. I have a few remarkably close and trusted friends, but at some point, they and I will fail one another. God does not fail. He is not a genie that can be ordered around, but He is faithful to be Himself, honor His word, and meet His obligations.

He blesses and provides for us all. Life, love, and sustenance are just the tip of the proverbial iceberg. He provides them through the creation, his servants as well as directly, when he chooses. If an honest person had a day to spend in identifying and listing each and every blessing God provides on a daily basis, they would be exhausted before they enumerated half of the list. (Try to thank Him as much as He blesses, - and you will be exhausted also.) Many of His blessings benefit the sinner as well as the righteous.

As a loving Father would teach, train, and discipline a child, God shows us the same love. To disciple or discipline is to reinforce some thinking/behavior and extinguish or realign others. A parent who does not set boundaries, teach morals, or educate a child socially is not doing their job. God does His job!

Face it. We can be mean. We sometimes rebel. We sin, hurt, damage, covet, and act in unbecoming ways all too often. But if you belong to Him, ask sincerely and intend to live better in the future (repent), He forgives. In fact, he patiently waits on most of us for long periods, hoping we will repent and seek forgiveness.

If the Old Testament relationship between Israel and Yahweh is closely reviewed, you see love, law, rules, and relationship. When Israel was obedient and loving, God blessed and rewarded. When they were defiant, disobedient, and unloving, God would warn, wait, and desire their repentance. But as patient as He was, His patience would eventually end, and punishment would occur. This pattern was repeated numerous times until God removed His Spirit from the Ark of the Covenant (Ezekiel 10) and Israel was enslaved and the prophets disappeared. For about four hundred years, the eternal did not speak. Why? Israel had quit listening. God's people were now dispersed, conquered, and left to suffer the consequence of disobedience. YAHWEH still loved them. They had quit loving Him—big mistake.

God is three (Trinity).

GOD DOES MIRACLES

As if creation were not enough, God has a habit of doing miracles or awesome events that many would call wonders. Now this is not the illusion or magic variety that showmen, charlatans, and illusionists practice. Who doesn't love it when Penn and Teller catch bullets with their teeth, David Copperfield makes a jet disappear, and Criss Angel appears to levitate in front of your eyes? They are illusions that take our breath away, but they are *not* miracles.

God doesn't use smoke, mirrors, misdirection, or any other staged tricks. When He turns water into blood, divides a sea so people can walk on dry land, or float an axe head on water, He does it by the word of His mouth or the activity of a servant. Having all authority over gravity, life, the periodic table, wind (you name it, He's in charge), they respond to His desire. Ponder the sun/time stopping so Israel can win a battle (Joshua 10), authority over the earth rotation and gravity. Dwell on (Ex. 17) striking a rock in a dry wilderness area that brings forth enough water for approximately 2.5 million people, livestock, and other needs. His authority is over fountains of the deep and where they appear.

Another difference between God's miraculous acts and a magician's illusion is that God's miracles have a purpose beyond making money or dazzling folks. His wonders tend to do the following: They are unmistakable signs that Yahweh and only He is behind it. They show the world that there is only one true God. God's snake eats all other snakes around (Ex. 7). When he uses an emissary like Moses, Elijah, or Daniel to witness, God does the miracles to show they are from God. They glorify Him and Him alone.

God still does miracles today. They are seldom as dramatic as the Old Testament biggies, but He now works in a subtler way. He is known to the world, in that 90-95 percent of all people believe in _a_ God. Those few that claim atheism rarely claim to have held that position all their life and many recant at some point in life. Regardless, "an exception to the rule does not change the rule." No, most believe in a god but not all believe in *the* God. After the death and resurrection of Jesus, most miracles recorded are done by the apostles and a few who were granted special gifts. Today most miracles are the result of faith, prayer, and the Holy Spirit acting upon or through someone on a limited basis. God often works through people His activities to perform. More on this topic under the title of the Holy Spirit.

The miracles seen today still illuminate His glory, can only be attributed to His intervention, and dazzle on a smaller scale than dividing the Red Sea (Ex. 14). But they are still miracles, like after prayer, dead people returning to life without a medical explanation; stage 4 cancer victims on the verge of death being cancer free in a matter of weeks; exact amounts of money arriving from unknown sources at the last moment (never early); and the list goes on.

I've prayed for many of these and have witnessed a considerable number. Nearly all have benefited Christians or Christian efforts, although when God calls someone to come to Him, He has been known to get their attention with an act that cannot be explained other than by God's direct intervention. He is not a genie in a bottle or Santa wanting to please children. But as the loving Father, He is involved in His kids' lives, so He knows it helps us to see Him working. He gives us a peek every now and then. (It helps to believe in Him as, otherwise, people look for coincidence or less likely explanations.)

I know this section is tough to accept, especially if you have asked and did not get the miracle you requested. Please do not lose heart. His ways are higher, and His thoughts are beyond what we are capable of thinking. I will not be able to satisfy your request to understand why, but if you have faith and trust as you study His word. It will become clear at some point.

Now some of you are wondering, maybe even perplexed, as to why I would seemingly close this script and then bring up miracles. You might think, "He's not a good writer." (My mom would be proud of this.) Others might say, "He is a rookie and needed more training." (Rookie, yes; need more training, absolutely!) Try this on for size: I am a poor writer, rookie, need more training, and yet though this might be the best way to introduce the next chapter, yes, the one about Jesus.

After four hundred years of silence, Yahweh will send the *Word*, and He will live among us. It is time for miracles and wonders once more to be performed, this time by a Deity in flesh and also through the power of the Holy Spirit. God (Jesus) who gave up His heavenly glory to live a human existence perfectly.

Stay tuned. More to come.

CHAPTER THREE

Jesus

God is one; God is trinity. Jesus is God! Accept this for now and let it simmer. This portion of the book is dedicated to the same folks as part one. It is to acquaint people with the God of the Bible. Many people in this world do not know the God of scripture. They may have heard of Jesus but have extraordinarily little accurate knowledge of who He is, much less His mission on earth, His lineage, His teachings, or His miracles. Unlike YHWH, who atheists and agnostics deny or doubt, it is hard to deny Jesus's existence. There is too much evidence and so much impact to ignore that He lived and was amazing. So many people will call Him a good person, teacher, philosopher, but never accept Him as God or our Savior. Scripture is clear that Jesus is also God and appeared in human form to experience life as we do. More than that, He did so to show us YHWH in all respects. His holiness, love, justice, and righteous life portrayed as He wishes us to live. So as we go down this path to learn about Jesus, remember we are seeing God as He was/is in the flesh.

Genesis 1:1-2, 26: "In the beginning, God created the heavens and the earth. The earth was without form and void, and darkness was over the face of the deep. And the Spirit of God was hovering over the face of the waters . . . Then God said, 'Let Us make man in our image, after our likeness. And let them have dominion over the fish of the sea and over the birds of the heavens and over the livestock and over all the earth and over every creeping thing that creeps on the earth.'"

John 1:1-3, 14: "In the beginning was the Word, and the Word was with God, and the Word was God. He was in the beginning with God. All things were made through him, and without him was not anything made that was made . . . And the Word became flesh and dwelt among us, and we have seen his glory, glory as of the only Son from the Father, full of grace and truth."

Luke 1:21-23: "'She will bear a son, and you shall call his name Jesus, for he will save his people from their sins.' All this took place to fulfill what the Lord had spoken by the prophet: 'Behold, the virgin shall conceive and bear a son, and they shall call his name Immanuel (which means, God with us).'"

John 10:28-30: "I give them eternal life, and they will never perish, and no one will snatch them out of my hand. My Father, who has given them to me, is greater than all, and no one is able to snatch them out of the Father's hand. I and the Father are one."

John 14:6-7, 10-11: "Jesus said to him, 'I am the way, and the truth, and the life. No one comes to the Father except through me. If you had known me, you would have known my Father also. From now on you do know him and have seen him . . .' Do you not believe that I am in the Father and the Father is in me? The words that I say to you I do not speak on my own authority, but the Father who dwells in me does his works. Believe me that I am in the Father and the Father is in me, or else believe on account of the works themselves."

There are many more verses in the Old and New Testaments that prophesy, or state Jesus is God. In these verses, he is referred to as God the Son or various other names and titles.

Okay, time for another amazing truth about Jesus. Not only is Jesus God, but He is also fully human—two completely different natures or persons in one body; fully God, fully human, fully flesh, and fully divine. He could bleed and heal wounds. He got hungry yet could feed thousands at one meal. Mark 4:35-41 is one passage that will make it easy to see both parts in one episode:

> 35On that day, when evening had come, he said to them, "Let us go across to the other side." 36And leaving the crowd, they took him with them in the boat, just as he was. And other boats were with him. 37And a great windstorm arose, and the waves were breaking into the boat, so that

the boat was already filling. [38]But he was in the stern, asleep on the cushion. And they woke him and said to him, "Teacher, do you not care that we are perishing?" [39]And he awoke and rebuked the wind and said to the sea, "Peace! Be still!" And the wind ceased, and there was a great calm. [40]He said to them, "Why are you so afraid? Have you still no faith?" [41]And they were filled with great fear and said to one another, "Who then is this, that even the wind and the sea obey him?"

He speaks as a man, and people take Him on a boat ride. A deadly storm threatens, and most get scared, while Jesus sleeps undisturbed. His followers, in terror, wake Him, the divine speaks, and the creation responds, both natures in one being, completely able to experience life as we do and yet retaining all the majesty and power of God.

Many years ago, the church fathers met and, after study, discussion, and agreement, wrote what is now known as the Chalcedonian Creed. The very scholarly result based on scripture explains in detail why they came to this conclusion. I urge you, at some point in the future, to ask a minister or Bible scholar to explain it more thoroughly than I have here; even better, do your own research before or after that conversation to make it more meaningful.

So in the beginning, Jesus is creator. As the infant and later young adult son of Mary and Joseph, he became fully human. He hurt when he stubbed his toe and laughed at a clean Joke. In this form, he was completely like us. His eternal divinity became visible in resurrected form; still a fully human appearance, but the new body He inhabits, has less restrictions than ours. He can walk through walls, appear in various recognizable and unrecognizable looks, and yet retained the pierced hands and side. Jesus is a man/God, living in heaven, seated at the right hand of God the Father. As I heard a minister state one time, "Jesus is our man in heaven." God is one, God is Trinity, and as such, Jesus is God.

Jesus Is God, Second Part of the Trinity

I know this may seem a bit redundant after the last section. Maybe it is, but it is short, and the purpose is to refocus the reader on the Trinity: God the Father, Jesus or God the son, and God the Holy Spirit.

Genesis 1:26-27 "Then God said, "Let us make man in our image, after our likeness. And let them have dominion over the fish of the sea and over the birds of the heavens and over the livestock and over all the earth and over every creeping thing that creeps on the earth. 27 So God created man in his own image, in the image of God he created him; male and female he created them.

In verse 26, when God says, "Let us . . .," God is not listing by name the three parts of the Trinity, but He is referring to the whole/unity of God. Jesus is God but with some roles shared with YWHW and the Holy Spirit. Other roles or functions are reserved to Himself. That does not impugn Him as God. Jesus is God the Son. Remember the water example. Steam and ice are water, the same as liquid, except it appears in a different presentation. Most of you think of YWHW first, the same as we think of liquid before steam or ice. It does not change the substance, just the presentation. Our thinking is normal as we see and interact more with the liquid. We think of God the Father or YHWH more than Jesus or the Holy Spirit as we lump all three in one, which is appropriate.

Besides the presentation, there is also a difference in role or function. Scripture often refers to Yahweh as the Father, Jesus as the Son or Son of God, and the Holy Spirit as the Spirit of God. God the Father sends Jesus and the Holy Spirit to do their activities. Mary is impregnated by the Holy Spirit with the seed that was Jesus. The Holy Spirit appears throughout the Old Testament as the agent of God that was "upon" prophets, judges, warriors, and kings, guiding or empowering them to do His will. Jesus said He would send the "Comforter" (Holy Spirit) to the disciples after His ascension. And He did, not to be "upon" people, but to live "within" those who accept the gift of salvation and obey the words of Jesus. Apostle Paul calls the Holy Spirit our "seal of redemption" until Jesus returns.

Jesus's role, among others, was to live a sin-free life, fulfill the law, carry *our* sins to the cross, and be *our* sin sacrifice, thus reconciling our debt to God, enacting justice, transforming sinners to righteousness, and restoring the relationship lost in the Garden of Eden. He did so willingly

———

as a human, feeling all the pain and anguish you or I would in the same situation. Other activities He fulfilled, including removing the need for a Levitical priesthood, allow Christians now to pray, confess sin, and bless God directly through the Holy Spirit. He also showed us Yahweh's attributes, character, and behavior since He was the image of God in flesh. He also began His church and trained over one hundred people at various levels to build it in preparation for His return. He had many disciples, but twelve were chosen specifically to be witnesses to the world after Jesus's death. (Side note: They and others did exactly as directed. Within a few years after Jesus returned to heaven, the "good news" (the gospel) had been preached throughout the world.)

Jesus is God, the second part of the Trinity.

Shared Characteristics of Jesus and God

As God, Jesus possesses the identical attributes, qualities, and traits of the Father. He was/is a Creator, all-knowing, all-powerful, ever-present, loving, blessing, and just God. If you go through the list of God's names, traits, and characteristics from part one of this book, you can find most as examples in the New Testament scripture exemplified by Jesus or testified to by His people. The following are just a few examples:

Yahweh (Father God)	Jesus (Son of God)
I Am "eternal and everlasting."	I Am "the Alpha and Omega."
All knowledge	"You know all things"
Holy	Anointed, set apart, pure
Unchanging	Same yesterday, now, in the future
Everywhere	Where Christians gather, I am there.
Completely powerful	All authority given to Him
Defines love	Went to the cross
Completely just	Determines who is His
Merciful	Died in our place for our sin

The list could continue, but the point is made. In the next pages, many examples will be drawn from scripture to show God as a human living righteously and sin free; not a good man, but a perfect man; not as an interpreter, but as author of scripture, life, and living; in some ways, enjoying the creation, but putting it in subjection as He chooses. When this chapter is complete, the reader will be left with a choice between two opposites: 1. Either Jesus is God and deserves our obedience and worship, *or 2.* many unrelated and unconnected people from over six thousand years contrived and pulled off *the* biggest hoax of all time. Beyond that, millions, if not billions, believed the hoax and accepted persecution, humiliation, torture, poverty, and martyrdom, trying to achieve the relationship with God that they desired. (#2 is *not* what happened!)

Hopefully, you have retained an open mind to scripture. Otherwise, you will fall for "the real hoax"—atheism. (Something came from nothing, somehow blew up, and we evolved from one-cell organisms into millions of particles, making up DNA that can walk, talk, and think up evolution of plants, insects, and animal species. By the way, they (proponents of no God) are never bothered by where the original matter came from as that doesn't fortify the snake oil they are selling. They confuse their theory of an eighteen-billion-year (or is it twelve or eight, it seems to change often) process with "compound interest". Put in one cell now and wait for billions of years, avoiding a market meltdown, a world will occur without a creator. Yeah, right!)

His-Story

A brief synopsis of Jesus before being human, as a human, and a glimpse of His future self; in Genesis, Jesus is alluded to from chapter 1 throughout the creation. We have already looked at many verses to this effect. He has the same Spirit form as YAHWEH and the Holy Spirit, with power and holiness just as the other two. Jesus was a part of the creation, wrestled with Jacob, and assisted the Israelites in their journey to Canaan. As such, he took on the form or appearance needed for the task.

In John 1, He is represented as the word, taking on flesh and living among us, just a regular guy, no special appearance or stature (Isaiah 53:2). He was diapered, bathed, and fed like any other child of the first century. I would not be surprised if He had acne, His voice broke during puberty, and He had to endure toothaches as we all have. This was His human nature and appearance until death on the cross and the resurrection.

After His resurrection, He walks the earth and is seen by 120 disciples and as many as 500 people total (1 Corinthians 15). Some of these people touched Him, questioned Him, ate with Him, and witnessed as He performed a few miracles (John 21). The idea was to make sure His disciples experienced Him in the flesh and could be eyewitnesses for future evangelism. In TV crime dramas, they often discount "eyewitness" testimony because, in a flash, people can be unsure or incorrect in identifying people, especially strangers. This is not the case with Jesus. He had people, His friends, and His disciples touch His wounds (John 20), eat a meal with Him, or engage Him in conversation so they could be absolutely sure of His identity.

After forty or so days of walking and meeting these hundreds of people, He takes the twelve out to a mount where He said goodbye and charged them with the task of making disciples. Then in their sight, He ascended to the skies and out of their sight (Acts 1:9-19). We are later told He is seated on the right-hand side of YAHWEH in heaven (Hebrews 8:1). The body there is recognizable and still in human form.

Let's not get stuck on appearance. It is the life He lived, the salvation He offered, and the gift He brought that needs our attention. Jesus's number one concern was not to impress us with Himself but, rather, to reveal YAHWEH to us and make atonement for our sins so we could be reconciled to God. Summarized, He came to save us from our sin, which would build His church and while at it, destroy the power of death.

Jesus Preached, Taught, and Prophesied

For a complete view of his teachings, read Matthew, Mark, Luke, and John. I do not plan to rewrite the gospels. Let me simply summarize one instant when He is teaching His disciples as an example. The text following is called the "Sermon on the Mount" (Matthew 5-7).

The close of Matthew 4 finds Jesus healing all kinds of illnesses. He is healing paralytics, diseases, those various afflictions common even today. This was being done while He preached the gospel (think good news). People came from miles away, not only to hear this man, but also for the healings of self, family, and friends. Remember, there were no cars or rapid transit. They were traveling miles to be healed physically or to hear this "rabbi" teach about God and His desires. In other words, they were seeking healing for the soul. How far would you walk to restore your inner self?

In chapter 5, the sermon begins. Jesus goes on a mountain and begins teaching His disciples by talking about who are blessed. The humble and the meek are listed, along with those who mourn. Humble people have a proper perspective between their worth and God's, whereas the meek are extraordinarily strong but have harnessed that strength in a positive way. He goes on basically praising people who have a righteous outlook on God, themselves, and their neighbors. This section closes with Jesus supporting those suffering for God's sake now because they will be rewarded in heaven. Remember, He is teaching His disciples.

Next, He compares his disciples to salt and light. Many a sermon has been preached on the various uses of salt two thousand years ago: taste enhancement, preservative for meats, its value as barter in a time when there were no accepted solid monetary valuation systems from country to country. Salt made a difference in people's lives as did a disciple of Jesus. When salt loses its "saltiness," it is not worth anything. So is a disciple who quits or gives up acting as a disciple.

Light was a wonderful metaphor for the attraction and clarity to be gained by His disciple. A follower of the Christ (Jesus as the anointed one of God) would be a light to direct/attract people to Jesus. Not only that, but His followers also should not hide or shade this light. They should be open and attracting to others. Remember, He is teaching His disciples.

Beginning in verse 17, we see the importance of the "law." The law of Moses is found in the Old Testament books of Exodus, Leviticus,

Numbers, and Deuteronomy. (Note; do not confuse the "Old Law" with the Old Testament. The old law is contained in the Old Testament but there is much more scripture for us to learn than just what the law of Moses contained.) Jesus came to fulfill the law of Moses. No one had ever been able to live sin free, so Jesus came to do this and free us of this burden by substituting Himself for us. That does not mean that there is no law and we can sin without consequence but that Jesus did what we could not. (This will get clearer as we go.) He calls His disciples to be more righteous than the religious leaders of His day some 2000 years ago.

Jesus expands the commandment against murder by showing that anger against a brother can lead to severe consequences. He implores us to work things out between ourselves rather than leave it up to the courts, etc. What is remarkable in these verses is that Jesus says working out this issue is more urgent than worshipping God. After we go to the brother and remedy the matter, *then* go worship. Worshipping God is important, so if Jesus says settle the matter first, you can see that He values a clear conscience and righteous relationships with others when you come to worship.

Next, Jesus confirms adultery as sin, and planning or setting it up is also sin even if you do not complete the act. Why? Because you intended to do it and would if the opportunity arose. Being whole spiritually is more important than being whole physically. Remember, He is teaching His disciples.

Jesus reiterated divorce as sin and with the exception of sexual immorality on the spouse's part, did not excuse the behavior. He went on to say that divorce for other reasons can lead to innocent parties becoming adulterers in subsequent marriages. As many will testify, divorce causes much pain, especially to children and other family members. Some people have interpreted these and other divorce passages to mean that Jesus will not forgive divorce for other reasons than adultery. Those people have forgotten that God forgives sin when the person requesting is sincere in their regret and shows Godly sorrow. In fact, when He forgives a sin, He also "forgets" the sin (Hebrews 10:11-18). The psalmist David wrote in Psalm 103 that forgiveness puts our sin as "far as the east is from the west."

Rather than swear an oath, Jesus wants us to be a person of integrity. Our word alone should be enough. This integrity extends to turning the other cheek, going out of your way, or being mistreated rather than pursuing revenge. Many people see this as unrealistic. Please keep it in perspective. These examples given are mild offenses, not life and death. He did not say let a thug beat you up every day or steal all your clothes. He is saying that to seek revenge for every offense is not the way of a disciple. Remember, He is teaching His disciples.

Chapter 5 closes with a plea to love and pray for our enemies. Anyone can love a friend; righteousness includes loving the unlovable. When we forgive others and pray for them, we are being like God. God loves all of us and forgives us, when requested, of all sin. If we are to be Godly, righteous, and holy, we need to act like God. When giving into our base mentality, we simply "up the ante" for part two of the conflict. If you are going to change an enemy into a friend, you best treat them as a friend. "People rarely act better when treated badly" is a quote I developed years ago in another time of my life. I find it holds merit today.

In chapter 6, Jesus gives other ways to be righteous. Give to the poor with a right heart, seeking the secret approval of God over the public praise of people. Pray in secret or in a private way. That way, God is honored and your relationship is unquestioned.

Jesus gives instructions on how to pray, and the theme is humility, not grandiosity. Honor God, acknowledge His sovereignty, request our daily physical needs. Then request forgiveness for your sins and failures and feel free to request protection or safety. The Messiah then gives a particularly important piece of information, critical to his disciple's spiritual growth. God will use our pattern or rule of forgiveness as His guide to when and how to forgive us. This is heavy-duty stuff. Let's say I refuse to forgive an insult or mistreatment; I have given God permission to choose not to forgive me the same trespass. Remember, He is teaching His disciples.

He closes chapter 6 with admonitions against worry and anxiety. He says *don't*! Worry and anxiety gain us nothing and cost us much. God cares, and He provides, so Jesus's message is to rely on God. The animals are provided for, and He loves us much more than the animals. Instead, focus on God and on becoming righteous. The benefit of this is to receive the needs of this world and a better life ahead.

In chapter 7, we are told to focus on our own sin and eliminate it prior to focusing on others' sins. Do not be a hypocrite. The amusing part is that we are described as having a pole in our eye while judging someone else over a spec in their eye. Many people have misused this verse to say that we are never to judge/condemn others. But when you read *all* of the New Testament, you will find that is not completely true. There are times when pointing out another person's sin is less about judging and more about encouraging the person. God has already made pretty clear what sin is, the consequences of violating his commands, and that Jesus will decide who is in the church and who is not. So to inform someone of the penalty in scripture is not to judge, but rather to warn, teach, or rebuke the sinner before it is too late. Verse 6 stuns many and bewilders others unfamiliar with the scripture. It is a deep and amazing statement. Jesus says do not waste the gospel on those who are adamantly refusing to leave sin and its filthy lifestyle. He says that they might not only demean the gift but also turn on you and attack you. Remember, He is teaching His disciples.

Other teachings include seeking and trusting the Heavenly Father for the things you need. Treat others as you wish to be treated, which is another way to say love one another. Realize the road to heaven is straight and narrow versus the highway to hell, which the majority of people choose for its wide lanes and illusion of easy living. He warns of false teachers who offer sweet fruit but never deliver. The lesson is simple: Good fruit comes from good trees, and bad fruit comes from diseased trees. Only follow those who deliver good fruit, i.e., "they walk the walk." On Judgment Day, the lawless will be separated from the true follower, even if they have some good works in their past.

Jesus closes the sermon on the mount with these thoughts: Build on a good foundation, and you can more easily withstand the storms of life. Build on an unstable foundation, and the storms will destroy your life. Jesus is the good foundation. Remember, He is teaching His disciples.

The people who were fortunate enough to hear Him teach His disciples were astounded by His ownership and passion. Think about it. Many came to see a miracle, to receive physical healing, to find out if this rabbi was really different in His message and power. And now they knew.

So why did the phrase "Remember, He is teaching His disciples" get repeated so many times? This was the pattern Jesus used in the first century. It was and is the pattern used today. Jesus taught His disciples, who taught His disciples, who continue generation after generation, many times over. The last three verses of Matthew 28 confirm the pattern and charge His disciples to continue this method. The gospel, the good news of Jesus the Christ, the Son of God, is to be shared so anyone who will hear, accept, and obey His message can be saved. Remember, He is teaching His disciples.

Jesus preached, taught, and prophesied.

JESUS OFTEN USED PARABLES

Parables are a unique form of storytelling. The gist of the story is about everyday life that people can relate to on a personal level. But there is a spiritual message buried or revealed in the narrative that teaches a much greater lesson to those who truly hear. Jesus used parables not only to fulfill prophesy but also to share insights with those who were true seekers of the kingdom. Some are more easily understood than others. Some required Him to explain to His disciples later as they missed the meaning entirely.

In Matthew 13, Jesus tells the parable of the sower. Condensed, it is how the gospel is received by four distinct groups. One group is hard ground and allows for no growth. One is shallow soil, which produces quick growth but without root structure, the plants quickly die. One soil is home to weeds and thistles, which quickly choke most of the seed to death. The last soil is fertile and produces a bumper crop.

This is a good example of how the world reacts to the message of Jesus. Some people never entertain the thought of a loving God and eternal life as a reward for faithful service. Sometimes people quickly accept the message, but without proper discipleship and support, they eventually give up. One group accepts the message, only to be choked out by the world's temptations, competing desires and other cares. The last group not only accepts the word but also acts. They respond to Jesus as their Savior and begin to grow a saving faith, live in obedience to Jesus's commands, and accept the life of glorifying God.

Other parables in this chapter describe the treasure of the kingdom of heaven. Other chapters of Matthew and the books of Mark, Luke, and John have a variety of parable topics. I will not go through all of them, but a couple of them are of special note.

In Luke 15 is the story of the prodigal son, his loving father, and his cynical elder brother. Concisely told, the younger brother brashly asks for his inheritance even before his father's death. His father concedes, and the youngster leaves to go live the high life. Quickly, a fool is separated from his money, and all his friends turn from him. Left homeless and living in a dumpster, he decides to humble himself and return home, seeking a servant's job. Dad is on the porch, hopeful for his return. When he spots him coming, Dad gives up all dignity in showing his joy for the boy's return. He runs to the lad, hugs him, clothes him, put shoes on his feet and jewelry on his finger. Happy, happy, happy, Dad throws a party. The elder brother hears of his brother's return, only to get angry, refusing to come to the party and pouting over the treatment his dad shows for the wasteful one. To top it off, he realizes Dad never threw him a party even though he was loyal to the old man. Dad tries to console him by reminding him that his reward is assured and he should be happy. His brother was back safe and sound. End of story. Not much of a story until it is applied to our spiritual self.

You see, the younger son represents many of us who have not become righteous. We want to live selfishly, as we choose, no matter what the cost. The elder brother represents those who follow the rules but do so out of reasons other than love and righteousness. Dad is a loving God who accepts our choices. He earnestly desires that we would come to Him and love Him as He loves us. He also wishes that the elder son would quit being so hard-hearted and become more loving so he could enjoy the kingdom already offered to him.

One other parable and I will end this section. That story is found in Matthew 20. It is one of my favorites, and soon, you will see why. A landowner needs help in his vineyard. He goes to the day labor headquarters and hires some guys for a mutually agreed salary of $100 for the day. Happily, they go to work. A couple of hours later, he hires some more folks for the same agreed wage. After lunch, he picks up a few more, and they agree to the same money. At 5:00 p.m., he picks up one more worker at the same mutually-agreed wage.

At quitting time, the owner pays each of them what they agreed to earlier. Wouldn't you know it, the guys hired at 8:00 a.m. were upset when he handed a $100 bill to them and the 1:00 p.m. and 5:00 p.m. workers. Upset, they started yelling, "This isn't fair."

"Fair? What is unfair?" asks the owner. "We agreed to this amount. What makes this unfair? It is my money, and I choose to pay the last the same as the first."

I know that if I worked all day for the same money as the 5:00 p.m. guy, I might also be ticked. But upon reflection, he, the owner, is right. I made an agreement to do such and such for $100, and that is all he owes me. Period. It is his money to use as he pleases. So the spiritual lesson is powerful. When we elect to serve God as a teen or when we turn eighty-seven years old, the agreement is between God and us.

I have no reason to question what the Sovereign Lord of creation does with, for, or to others. He is God. Period. Is it not refreshing, even encouraging, that God will call and accept us whenever we decide to show up for service? It destroys the excuse many have misused, "I am too old "or "It's is too late for me." As long as there is breath, there is hope.

To summarize the last two sections, Jesus was a master teacher. He came to teach, train, and empower disciples so they could make disciples who would make disciples, etc. This was His divine method for building His church, revealing the Father to the world, and reconciling us to God the Father.

It is interesting to me that people who live by His sermons and yet do not accept salvation still experience a more peaceful life than most of mankind. The same can be said for the life He lived. People who live a life like Jesus will end up helping more than hurting, loving more than hating, and being more accepted than rejected. Had He not claimed (rightfully) to be the Messiah and as such, threatened the religious rulers standing in power, I dare say He would have not been crucified. But that was not His task. Reconciliation was His task. The Jewish leaders could not accept Him in that role, so they lobbied for His death.

Jesus often used parables.

JESUS LIVED A WELL-PLANNED LIFE

The first three chapters of Matthew and Luke give us the little information we have on Jesus's arrival and early life. Jesus was born of a virgin who bore the disgrace of pregnancy before marriage at a time that this was reason for shame, shunning, and even death. Chosen by YAHWEH to be Jesus's mother, Mary willingly accepted the role. His foster father Joseph was also a righteous man who accepted the task of raising God's son and marrying Jesus's mother when, by law, he could have walked away from her and the scandal. Nothing is written of Jesus's life from age two until age twelve. Then again, nothing is written in scripture except for His occupation until approximately age thirty.

I cannot say definitively why God gave us so little information on His childhood. I suspect it was because it has nothing to do with reconciliation and the salvation He brought to the world. Also, it might distract us (sinners) from the message, sacrifice, and grace that He represents to all who believe in Him. Regardless, what we do know is what we need to know, to find and accept salvation. I am happy to settle my curiosity later, face to face, *if* it is still important to me. (I suspect it will not be in my top 10 list of questions.)

Now how to summarize His life (example) on earth as a pattern for us to follow? Let's start with just selecting one book and reviewing His behavior. Using Mark's gospel as our guide, we see that His ministry was announced by His cousin John the Baptist. When Jesus is proclaimed by John, people who had learned from John quickly chose to listen to Jesus.

First, He chose to be baptized and then immediately faced off against Satan in the wilderness. Here, we see two qualities from the beginning of His ministry. He shows humility by insisting on baptism before asking us to do the same. He was affirmed by YAHWEH and the Holy Spirit on the spot. Second, he shows courage by facing the devil on His own turf. In resisting the temptations of the accuser, he is now ready to begin his ministry.

He proclaimed it was time to repent, for the kingdom of God was here. This is bravery, risking scorn to preach such a message. In doing so, some people were attracted to Him and His message. From those people, He began to identify and call disciples. While in the synagogue, He was identified by a demon-possessed man as the holy one of God. Jesus immediately exorcises the demon and amazes the people with His authority and teaching. Notice he is now acting as God on earth, and many miracles followed. Capernaum became His most frequent base, but He traveled to many towns, and His fame spread.

It seems His methodology was to heal people and perform miracles, then teach or preach, and then go to the next location. Often His sermons began with a question from which He answered with spiritual truth. He showed pity and compassion to a leprous person who told everyone, although asked to keep quiet. This and other miracles made it difficult for Him to appear in metropolitan areas, so He often stayed in wilderness areas and other sparsely-settled places. The people then came to Him. (Think about that.)

In Mark 2, we see Him continue these behaviors, but now the crowds are larger, and some religious leaders start coming to see this non-traditional "rabbi" and challenge him on his teachings. Jesus heals a paralytic by saying, "Your sins are forgiven." The leaders are stunned because only God can forgive sin, and here, a carpenter's son, is using divine language. To their challenge, Jesus deflects by saying, it is as easy to say, "Your sins are forgiven" as "Take up your bed and walk."

Later Jesus eats with sinners. Criticized for doing so, He replies that He came for the sinners, not the righteous. (Ponder that remark.) Fasting is a self-imposed restriction of food or drink for a specific time period. Many Jews practiced this spiritual restriction. When asked why His disciples did not fast like they did, He answered in spiritual terms that His presence was like a wedding party, and no one fasts at a party. Also, mixing the old with the new seldom works, especially when you try to put the new into the old. Deep stuff, but they were not ready yet for meaty truths, so He shared it with them a little at a time. Lastly, in this chapter, He was challenged about His disciples breaking some dietary rules of the rulers. He asserted His authority as Lord of the Sabbath and explained the Sabbath is for us and not us for the Sabbath.

Chapter 3 follows with more challenges and more wisdom from Jesus. The twelve disciples are named, verses 16-19. From this time on, they become near-constant companions until His death. Jesus continues to irk the religious leaders by ignoring or invalidating some of their traditions, teaching that the Sabbath is a time for doing good, that healing is more important than stifling rules, and giving them the warning about blaspheming the Holy Spirit. The common or ordinary people are now following Him in droves.

Chapter 4 is full of parables. It closes with Jesus commanding a storm to stop, and it does. Fearless in the face of death, criticism, or spite, Jesus is living love toward His followers and critics alike.

In chapter 5, two amazing stories unfold. First, he travels to a place where a demon-possessed man is terrorizing the local population. Jesus frees him from a "legion" (a whole bunch) of demons by sending them into a herd of pigs. Witnesses tell the owners of the pigs what happened. They insist Jesus leave, and he consents. The newly demon-freed man asks to go with Jesus. Jesus says no but gives him a missionary's task of going to tell others what God had done for him. Think about it. One, Jesus freed a demon-possessed man, and yet the pig owners do not want to spend time with Him. Two, the formerly-possessed man is wanting to travel with Jesus, yet Jesus puts him to work with only his story to tell, no training, no theological courses, just tell your story of what God has done for you. Three, Jesus leaves as requested. No punishment for the pig owners, no ego-trip over being asked to leave. It is as if Jesus only came to the graveyard to free one and inform many, and then he left.

The second story has two parts. He is asked to come heal a sick child. On the way, He is touched by a lady with an unclean disease. In that day and time, she would not have been accepted in public with this disease, yet she was desperate to be healed. Her faith that Jesus could heal her forced her to break the rules. She touched His garment and was well instantly. Jesus felt the impact and wanted to know who had touched Him. She confessed, and He praised her faith. Arriving at the little girl's home, He is told that it is too late. The child is dead. Pay attention! God is never too late. He is always right on time! Excusing everyone unnecessary from the room, He raises this child from death to life. This is the first of several death sentences He postpones while on earth. Now that is God at work.

Mark 6 will amaze all who read with an open mind and accepting heart. This Jesus is showing YAHWEH in the flesh and the love He has for us. Oddly, it begins with rejection. Jesus returns to the village of His childhood and early adulthood. He returns as the Messiah, but the people could not fathom Him other than as the carpenter's son. They know his four brothers and all his sisters. Yet like us, they cannot get past who they believed Him to be, to see Him as He really was. He taught in the synagogue, but rather than "hear" and "see" truth, they seek the familiar, who they assumed Him to be, rather than what and who He was in truth. I grew up with many high school friends and acquaintances. After years of separation, I was astounded to learn that the quiet kid was now a Doctor, the non-conformist was into electronics and computers, one of the beauty queens actually knew my name, and an underclassman became a just, yet compassionate, judge. We all struggle taking a second look, and so did the people of Nazareth. Jesus is deflated and states a continuing truth. In verse 4, he is quoted, "A prophet is not without honor, except in his hometown and among his relatives and in his own household."

He sends out His disciples to share the good news and gives them instruction about what to take, where to stay, and what to do. He also empowered them to do some amazing things. Upon return, they shared stories of healing and other miracles. Remember, He is teaching His disciples.

As Jesus's fame grows, His reputation reached the king of the land. Worried that this Jesus was actually John the Baptist returning from the dead, Herod inquired about Jesus. A guilty conscience causes this kind of anxiety.

Soon there is another crowd gathered to see the miracles and hear the gospel of the Christ. They remained for a long time, so Jesus, in compassion, decides to teach His disciples another lesson. He tells them to feed the multitude. They can't, and then Jesus does. Using the lunch of one kid, Jesus makes it into a banquet for thousands. The disciples take the food from Jesus's hands and puts it into the people's hands, and all are fed. With leftovers. See the pattern? Remember, He is teaching His disciples.

The chapter closes with two incidents of note. Jesus and His disciples are separated for a time, and he meets them later on the boat they are rowing. Of course, He walks on the water to the boat. To the Lord of creation, it is no big thing to walk on water, much less to still the wind with a word. You see, the disciples are still struggling with who He is, and they didn't "get it" even after the feeding of thousands with two fish and a little bread. Does this remind you of, oh, say the world? Next, He goes to the Gennesaret. People recognize Him and come a-running. Do you wonder if it might have to do with a demon-possessed man turned missionary?

Mark 7 has a variety of teachings. One thing to notice is Jesus's disdain for the hypocrites that served in religious leadership. Verses 1-13 speak of a tradition these leaders taught. They said that if you gave gifts to the temple, you were relieved of supporting your parent when they were in need. This is in direct contradiction to the fifth commandment (Exodus 20:12). Then He reminds them that the prophets of old had predicted this type of instruction would take place. He says they do many things that negate the commands of God in favor of their own teachings.

Next, Jesus explains that the food and drink we consume do not defile us as they are digested and leave the body. What does defile us is the hurtful things we say. They come from the heart and mind. As such, they show unrighteousness by hurting others who are also made in the image of God.

Verses 24-30 may shock you unless first you understand a truth. Whatever God decides is morally correct. The Israelites were the chosen people of God. His plan of salvation for mankind specifically used the nation born through the patriarchs Abraham, Isaac, and Jacob. (Read the book of Genesis for more in-depth knowledge.) Long story made short is that their children and families ended up living in Egypt for over four hundred years. They grew from about seventy people to approximately 2.5 million or a small nation. God, using Moses, brought them out of bondage in Egypt to the promised land. They became the chosen nation of God and received the law of Moses.

Jesus is God. These are his people spiritually, physically, by covenant, by human linage, and by choice. The Messiah Jesus was here to first reclaim Israel and second humanity. So when he uses the analogy of Jews as children of God and the gentiles as dogs, he is referring to their status before God, big versus Little, family versus outsiders. Does it sound insulting and hurtful to us today? Yes, *if* we do not understand that God is sovereign, holy, righteous, and the creator. As such, he loves this Syrophoenician lady, but she is not of his chosen people. The people of his day would understand the analogy. She, at that time, was part of a lost world. So when she asked for her daughter to be healed, Jesus reply is He is here to heal the Jews first. Give her credit. She took His words and applied them literally, gaining His respect and a miracle healing for Her daughter. Most of us would have argued or insulted Him. We, in the last few years, have lost the ability to understand and accept that not every culture views analogies, metaphors, and similes with the critically sensitive nature currently popular. Should you call people dogs in today's climate? No. Did this lady respond the way we do today? No. It appears she got the point and the miracle. Can you?

The chapter closes with Jesus healing a deaf/mute person. He then instructs him to keep the miracle quiet. Of course, the healed one cannot contain his joy and tells everyone. Was Jesus using a crude paradox to get more attention? Or rather, was He sincere because it was difficult going anywhere without being mobbed? You decide. Scripture tells us what we need to know, not all we would like to know.

Chapter 8 includes another picnic for four thousand people. Jesus views the crowd with compassion and feeds them with seven loaves of bread and a few fish. Leftovers, seven baskets. It is most important to notice that His disciples wonder from where the food will come. How quickly have they forgotten what Jesus can do? They continue to think logically and ignore that God has no limits (except the self-imposed). They still do not get it. Jesus is God. We are much the same way. Never judge what God can or will do by human standards. We are made in His image, not the other way….. Oh, you know.

In verses 11-13, the Pharisees (one sect of religious leaders) demand Jesus to do a miracle in their presence. He refuses and leaves. In the other gospels, this is repeated, always with the same response. Jesus is not here to do parlor tricks. He is on mission, and the Pharisees simply need to observe what He does, listen to His sermons, and then determine if He is the real thing, become followers and see it all. Hum, that must have escaped them. When people already have their minds made up, why bother observing with an open mind? I cannot confirm the source, but when learning tennis in college, a friend said, "If you are going to call the ball out of bounds, why bother looking?" I later asked him if that was an original line. He said he thought it was first said by tennis legend Tony Trabert. I spent a few minutes trying to confirm the source without success. Regardless of the origin, it is a great example of a closed mind or protecting a personal agenda by ignoring the truth.

Leven (yeast) is used in baking to make flour rise. It is a foreign substance added to the recipe that changes the product's appearance, taste, and texture. In verses 14-21, Jesus teaches His disciples using this example. "Beware" of the Leven of the Pharisees and King Herod. The good news of Jesus will be changed by those who do not respect God's words. It happened then, and it happens now. People will add to or remove God's meaning to suit their agenda.

Healing the blind had never been done in the history of Old Testament. In verses 22-26, Jesus does what had never been done before. Some critics will ask, "How come it took two attempts to get it right?" I bet the formerly-blind man was not bothered by this even a little bit.

In verses 27-29, Jesus asks His disciples two critical questions: (1) Who do people say I Am? They gave him a variety of answers. (2) Who do you say I Am? Peter responds, "You are the Messiah!" It is important to realize that today, we, have to determine the same truth. We also will need to personally confess Jesus as the Messiah, the Son of God.

Speaking clearly (versus 30-38), Jesus tells of the suffering and death He will experience. Peter tries to stop Him, and Jesus calls him Satan. Why? Peter does not yet understand the mission of Jesus completely. He wants Jesus to use His power in other ways. The disciple should never correct the master about the master's goal. Humility requires we ask, not tell. Servants obey, not argue. God is to be obeyed, not advised. We must remember who He is and who we are not!

"The Transfiguration" (chapter 9) is a title given to a unique happening. Jesus took Peter, James, and John, his three closest disciples, to a mount away from the crowds and other disciples. From the grave appeared Moses and Elijah, both chatting with Jesus. Jesus's clothing changed into an ultra-white garment, and the three disciples were afraid. Peter, always the first to speak, suggested they build tents/tabernacles to honor the prophets and Jesus. Clouds appear. YAHWEH's voice is heard clearly: "This is my beloved Son; listen to him." Friends, God is being as transparent as an invisible deity may. Moses's and Elijah's times are past. They both knew of him from Father God but now His Son and no one else is to be heard. There are many lessons in this passage, but we will remember what God said first and foremost. "This is my beloved Son; listen to him." That is enough to be said! In the following verses, Jesus tells them to keep this on the "QT" until after His resurrection. He also explains the prophesy of Elijah paving the way, (restoring things) for Jesus was already fulfilled. In other gospels, He refers to John the Baptist filling that role.

In the narratives that follow, He heals a demon-possessed child and explains that greatness in the kingdom of heaven is measured by humility and service, not by human standards. He explained that those not against Him are actually for HIM. And people who help His disciples will be rewarded for their acts of kindness. He closes with a short lesson on temptation. If someone causes a believer (disciple) to sin, they will be punished severely. He expands this to include anything that would keep someone from the kingdom of Heaven. In emphasis, Jesus even states that to remove a body part that causes temptation is preferable to missing heaven.

Chapter 10 begins with a short lesson in what God intended marriage to be: one man, one woman, for life. Under the old law, Moses had allowed divorce caused by the meanness of some husbands to allow women to survive when she was no longer wanted. That often led to adultery by an otherwise innocent party. However, Jesus also was incredibly open to children and warned others to not hinder their approaching Him. Verses 17-21 tells the story of a righteous young man who was rich. He followed the law of Moses and asked what else he needed to do for eternal life. In love, Jesus said that the only thing hindering him was his love of money. The young man walked away sad. The bigger story is in the next few verses as Jesus explains that the wealthy will find it impossible to enter heaven on their own, but God can and will make it possible for some to do so. It is a matter of love and obedience. If we love money more than God, the kingdom is beyond our reach. But the person who puts God first will be rewarded greatly in this life and in the next (not always financially). God can and will do for His people what we can never do on our own.

Jesus then shares with the disciples a third time of His impending arrest, death, and resurrection. You might wonder why the twelve need to be told this same thing many times. Then remember how often your parents warned you of future problems, and you really did not get it. It is human nature to sluff off the bad when things are going well. James and John, two of Jesus's favorite disciples, made a request, basically asking to be appointed to high positions when Jesus entered His kingdom. It would be like asking the president of the country to be secretary of state or White House chief of staff. Jesus made it clear those two positions were not His to grant. Only the Father chooses those officials. To be considered great in the future kingdom, you must become a servant to all, just like Jesus had. Jesus had authority to do as He wished, but His actions were always to serve, assist, heal, teach, and model righteousness. Jesus expected the same of His disciples.

The chapter closes with a particularly important lesson. Bartimaeus, a blind man, calls for help. The crowd tells him to hush because they do not want Jesus to be bothered by him. (Odd, people want Jesus to care for them but ignore others.) The blind one becomes more insistent. Jesus responds and asks, "What do you want?" Bart says, "I want to regain my sight." Jesus replies that his faith has made him well. Faith in Jesus is the most important attribute of Christians (Hebrews 11:6).

As stated earlier, Mark is the shortest of the four gospels. In chapter 11, we find Jesus entering Jerusalem on a colt as prophesied in the Old Testament. People are laying their clothes and palm branches on the ground for the colt to trod as they would for a king coming to town (think red carpet). Singing and praising God now for His gift of Jesus, how quickly things will change in the next week. He entered the temple and then left to get rest.

The next day, Jesus shows a side of Himself that people who do not know Him find it hard to accept. Being hungry and expecting figs on a nearby tree, He curses it when He finds it barren. Next, He arrives at the temple, only to find it being used as a sale barn, flea market or open-air business. He overturns the tables and runs off the merchants, even refusing people use of it as a pathway to other places. Teaching the people about the purpose of the temple, he showed contempt for those who used it as a marketplace.

That night He and His disciples left Jerusalem, but now the rulers of the temple are mad and looking for ways to kill him. Upon returning the next day, the disciples pass a dead fig tree. Peter remembers the curse from yesterday and remarks his surprise. Jesus again reminds them of faith's role in receiving from God the power to do miraculous wonders. The idea is that when you ask, do not doubt, but act as if it has already happened. He also reminded them that to forgive others encourages God to forgive them. Remember, He is teaching His disciples.

Later, in Jerusalem, temple leaders challenged His authority to teach and perform miracles. Jesus has a few more things to do before His crucifixion, so He turns their questions back on them. He asked where John the Baptist got his authority. Busted! The Temple leaders did not obey John. So to say God gave it to John would make them hypocrites for not obeying. On the other hand, the people knew John was from God, so they would be condemned if they denied John's ministry. Being good politicians (cowards), they pleaded the fifth (actually ignorance), and so Jesus refused to answer them.

Chapter 12 is full of great wisdom and lessons. Jesus tells a parable about a rich farmer who rents out his land for a percentage of crop income. Summarized, he sent several servants to collect the rent, but they were abused and or killed by the tenants, and no payment was rendered. As a last resort, he sent his son, expecting him to be respected. They did not and killed him as well. At this point, Jesus asked the listeners a rhetorical question, "What will the landowner do?" Answering it Himself, He predicted the tenants death, and the vineyard was given to those who would use it righteously. The religious leaders knew this parable was about them, and they wanted to lay hands on Jesus. However, they knew the crowds would not tolerate it as they believed in Jesus. So they tucked tail and disappeared for a while.

Jesus taught the crowd to pay their taxes while also tithing to God. Next, the Sadducees (another Jewish religious sect) try their luck at stumping Jesus. Unlike the other leaders of the religion (Pharisees), these guys did not believe in a future resurrection of the dead. In a very hypocritical way, they ask about marriage in the next life. (Attention, they do not even believe in a next life.) Jesus shoots them down in short order. He first explains that they really do not know the Old Testament scripture. Second, He tells them that they also do not know the power of God. (1) There is no marriage in heaven. (Men and women's need for each other on earth is explained in Genesis) (2) YAHWEH is God of the living, not the dead, speaking spiritually, so He is God of all the saved, from the beginning of time until Judgment Day and thereafter.

Next, Jesus makes it crystal clear for all to hear. The greatest command is to love God with all your being. The second is to love your neighbor as yourself. God wants this more than burned offerings or sacrifices. Jesus now poses a question that will cause people to think deeply: "How can the Messiah be the son of David when David calls Him LORD?" The answer is in two dimensions: Jesus was a descendant of King David by way of Mary, his mother's lineage. But as the Son of God, Holy Spirit-induced, he is LORD by spiritual lineage; born of flesh and Spirit. (By the way, the people present did not get the answer as you just did. They had to figure it out.)

His last warning of this chapter is pointed at the scribes (religious leaders who read and interpreted the scriptures). He points out that some are hypocrites who only want power, status, and money. They may look or act religious but take care to see who is making pretense as opposed to righteousness. As an example, he points out a widow who gives all she has, as opposed to those giving out of abundance.

Chapter 13 contains information about the end times. Jesus begins by prophesying the destruction of the temple, which would occur about thirty years post his resurrection. When four disciples ask for signs of the end of days, Jesus replies on several levels at once. Some predictions of false Christs coming, wars, famines, and natural disasters are mentioned. He then speaks to trials and events that the twelve and other disciples will face. Stating clearly that the gospel will be preached to the world, the disciples will testify in front of earthly powers, and the Holy Spirit will guide their replies and conversations.

Then shifting gears, He returns to a discourse about the beginning of the end. It will get bad. False Christs will appear, chaos and calamity will occur, and there will be much to fear. But God will call an end to the destruction early, so Christians who hold true can endure. After the tribulation, Jesus will return and have the angels gather His people to Him. He closes with encouragement that some will not die until some of these predictions come true. He closes this discourse with an admonition to remain alert and faithful because no one knows when the end will come. (We still do not)

Chapter 14 begins with a reminder that the religious leaders are still wanting to harm/kill Jesus. They fear the people and want to time their actions so as not to disrupt the Passover feast or bring reprisals on themselves. Meanwhile, Jesus is dining with a previous leper in the presence of disciples and friends. A woman anoints His feet with expensive ointment, much to the consternation (he was bothered) of a disciple. Jesus tells him to lay off. This lady is doing a nice thing for Jesus before His death, and she will be remembered for such. Using the price of the ointment would help a few poor folks, but you can always help the poor. She gets only this one opportunity to show love for Jesus prior to His death. Judas soon decides to betray Jesus and arranges the details with the religious leaders.

It's Thursday night, and Jesus wants to celebrate the Passover with the twelve. A room is prepared, the meal eaten, and then Jesus announces one of them as His betrayer. He later teaches a divine ritual still practiced by Christians this century. Scripture refers to it as the Lord's Supper, but it is also called communion or the eucharist by different groups. The purpose was to pause and remember Christ's sacrifice on a regular basis. It consisted of unleavened bread to represent his body and wine to remember the blood shed for our sins. They closed the meal by singing a hymn and departing to the mount of olives. Remember, He is teaching His disciples.

There, Jesus prophesied that the twelve would desert Him soon. Peter swore he would be there to the death. So did the rest. Jesus predicted the opposite and told Peter he would deny Jesus three times before the rooster (think alarm clock) crowed twice. He then sought YAHWEH in prayer while the others waited a short distance away. It's late night, and they went to sleep. Jesus pleaded with God to change His mind about the crucifixion but promised to go through with the plan if Father God so desired. Returning to the disciples, He woke them and pleaded for them to stay awake and pray. He prayed two more times, but both times, the disciples slept until He said it was time to go.

Judas arrived with a posse of the religious leaders, a scuffle ensued, and one fellow lost an ear as they arrested Jesus. Jesus's followers run away (one naked) as they took Jesus in for a kangaroo court run by the religious hierarchy. The witnesses could not agree on His "crimes" or their testimony. Things are going nowhere until, finally, a high priest asked Jesus if he was the Christ, the Son of God. He said yes and in the future, He would return in glory. They charged Him with blasphemy (claiming to be God) and started assaulting Him. Outside, Peter is trying to be inconspicuous as the trial proceeds. He is accused three times of being a Jesus follower, and he lies all three times. The rooster does as predicted, Peter realizes his sin, and in brokenness, he cries.

Mark 15 begins with a second trial. This time the governor of Judea, Pilate, presides. Pilate asks Jesus if He is the king of the Jews, and Jesus replies to the affirmative. Pilate tries to get out of this situation, but the priest and their supporters insist on crucifixion. Pilate has Jesus whipped and then allowed an innocent man to be murdered. First, the soldiers mock and beat Him, crown Him with thorns, and then took Him to the place of final demise. By 9:00 a.m., He was stripped, nailed to the cross, and His clothing used as the prize, for which the soldiers gambled to win.

A sign was posted declaring Him to be the king of the Jews. What irony? It ticked off the priest, was absolutely accurate, and Pilate, the sign author, had no idea what he had done. Jesus's enemies ridiculed Him while He was in pain, bystanders mocked Him, and even the two thieves dying to His left and right joined in the fun. By noon, the sky had turned dark and remained that way for three hours (no, not an eclipse). Around 3:00 p.m., Jesus, now in tremendous pain, forsaken by God, cries out in agony. They offer Him sour wine, which He refused, and then He died. The temple curtain, some distance away, tore from top to bottom, adding to the miracles of this day. Even the commanding soldier had to admit that Jesus was the Son of God. A few of the women, whom Jesus had previously ministered to when He was preaching, witnessed the end.

Hurriedly, He was wrapped in a clean linen, placed in a new tomb, and a huge stone placed in front of the opening. This was witnessed by Mary Magdalene and one other lady.

Chapter 16 finds several ladies going to Jesus's tomb after the Sabbath to give Jesus a proper burial with spices and to anoint the corpse. He was not there! The stone was moved, and they were told, "He is risen" by the angel. They were instructed to tell the apostles (and Peter) to meet him in Galilee. According to some scholars, this closes the book of Mark. Other ancient manuscripts add the following:

Jesus later met with Mary Magdalene and instructed her to tell the disciples He was alive. She did, but they did not believe her. Jesus met later with two disciples who, once they recognized Him, went to tell the others but were not believed. It took an appearance from Jesus Himself to convince them He was alive. He rebuked them for being so hardheaded. Later He gave them the commission to preach the gospel to the world. Those who believed and were baptized would be saved. Others would be lost. He closed by describing some of the miracles they would do in His name. He then went back home (heaven) and now sits on the right-hand side of God. And the disciples? Well, they did as he said. You see, we must remember He was here teaching His disciples, not only the twelve, but also all disciples of Jesus from then until the second coming of Jesus.

Let us summarize:

Jesus lived a well-planned life.

Jesus lived to show us what God is really like.

Jesus lived to seek and save the lost.

Jesus lived to reconcile man to God.

Jesus lived to fulfill the old law.

Jesus lived to become the perfect sacrifice to appease God's wrath.

Jesus lived as the grace of God, taking our place on the cross.

Jesus lived to build His church.

And to do all this, Jesus lived to teach His disciples so they could teach His disciples.

Jesus lived a well-planned life.

JESUS DIED ON THE CROSS

Jesus is God, and He is our Savior. We have seen in Mark just a glimpse of His love, compassion, and service for all humanity. Now we need to focus on the cross and its meaning in all this. For some, it is easy to think of the pain He must have endured and, in the next breath, dismiss its purpose and impact. For others, the pain and humiliation seem an overblown story to appease the masses, lure the ignorant, or increase our shame. We might ponder, "Why this type of sacrifice?" or "Why did God even come up a plan that involved killing His own son?" Surely there was another way. To paraphrase the movie *Airplane*, no, there was not a better way, and my name is not Shirley. God is holy, perfect in all His ways.

Since YAHWEH required unblemished sacrifices from His people, He required the same of Himself. Since he demanded the "first fruits" of the field, Jesus, the "Alpha," was the only possible offering. God wants perfection (holiness) from us, and yet He knew we could not deliver, so He sent perfection to us, for us, as a substitute offer of perfection. (1 John 2:2 "He is the propitiation for our sins, and not for ours only but also for the sins of the whole world". God loved the world (us) so much that he offered Jesus as perfection for our sins, blood for cleansing, forgiveness for sin, and life for death. In John 3:17 the disciple states we were *already* dead before Jesus came. He brought the hope of eternal life to all who believed and obeyed His words.

Please note the following scriptures and comments:

Colossians 1:19-20: "For in him all the fullness of God was pleased to dwell, and through him to reconcile to himself all things, whether on earth or in heaven, making peace by the blood of his cross."

Jesus reconciles us to God and God to us. His blood brings spiritual peace.

Colossians 2:9-14: "For in him (Jesus) the whole fullness of deity dwells bodily, and you have been filled in him, who is the head of all rule and authority. In him also you were circumcised with a circumcision made without hands, by putting off the body of the flesh, by the circumcision of Christ, having been buried with him in baptism, in which you were also raised with him through faith in the powerful working of God, who raised him from the dead. And you, who were dead in your trespasses and the uncircumcision of your flesh, God made alive together with him, having forgiven us all our trespasses, by canceling the record of debt that stood against us with its legal demands."

This He set aside, nailing it to the cross. Jesus releases us from the physical circumcision of the Jew and gives a spiritual circumcision. By baptism into Jesus and being raised in faith, it mimics the resurrection God performed on Jesus. He gives us the same "life" through forgiveness.

1 Corinthians 1:18-25: "For the word of the cross is folly to those who are perishing, but to us who are being saved it is the power of God. For it is written, 'I will destroy the wisdom of the wise, and the discernment of the discerning I will thwart.' Where is the one who is wise? Where is the scribe? Where is the debater of this age? Has not God made foolish the wisdom of the world? For since, in the wisdom of God, the world did not know God through wisdom, it pleased God through the folly of what we preach to save those who believe. For Jews demand signs and Greeks seek wisdom, but we preach Christ crucified, a stumbling block to Jews and folly to Gentiles, but to those who are called, both Jews and Greeks, Christ the power of God and the wisdom of God. For the foolishness of God is wiser than men, and the weakness of God is stronger than men."

People who do not recognize God often believe themselves to be wiser in spiritual matters than God or Christ followers. Since God knows all, He easily makes fools of the haughty. By the sacrifice of Jesus, the faithful, humble, and obedient to God are saved.

Philippians 2:5-11: "Have this mind among yourselves, which is yours in Christ Jesus, who, though he was in the form of God, did not count equality with God a thing to be grasped, but emptied himself, by taking the form of a servant, being born in the likeness of men. And being found in human form, he humbled himself by becoming obedient to the point of death, even death on a cross. Therefore God has highly exalted him and bestowed on him the name that is above every name, so that at the name of Jesus every knee should bow, in heaven and on earth and under the earth, and every tongue confess that Jesus Christ is Lord, to the glory of God the Father."

Again, confounding the "wise," Jesus humbled Himself and obediently came to earth as a man, accepting voluntary demotion from Creator to created. Since His death, burial, and resurrection, God has promoted this man back to His former status and elevated His name above all others. The "wise" of earth, angels, and demons alike will, in the future, bow to Jesus. How foolish the "wise" will feel when they grovel before the Christ alongside Satan and his crowd.

1 Peter 2:22-24: "He committed no sin, neither was deceit found in his

mouth. When he was reviled, he did not revile in return; when he suffered, he did not threaten, but continued entrusting himself to him who judges justly. He himself bore our sins in his body on the tree, that we might die to sin and live to righteousness. By his wounds you have been healed."

A sin-free man took our sin to the cross. He died in our place that we might "die" to sin. More than that, we can now live a righteous life in the pattern He set.

Hebrews 10:12-18: "But when Christ had offered for all time a single sacrifice for sins, he sat down at the right hand of God, waiting from that time until his enemies should be made a footstool for his feet. For by a single offering he has perfected for all time those who are being sanctified. And the Holy Spirit also bears witness to us; for after saying, 'This is the covenant that I will make with them after those days, declares the Lord: I will put my laws on their hearts, and write them on their minds,' then he adds, 'I will remember their sins and their lawless deeds no more.' Where there is forgiveness of these, there is no longer any offering for sin."

Jesus sits at God's right hand, waiting, waiting for those who would choose Him to do so and for evil to bow before His throne. People know right from wrong as the Holy Spirit says. Once saved, there is no reason to ask again. One death, for all, is sufficient for those who live the life of faith.

Hebrews 12:1-2: "Therefore, since we are surrounded by so great a cloud of witnesses, let us also lay aside every weight, and sin which clings so closely, and let us run with endurance the race that is set before us, looking to Jesus, the founder and perfecter of our faith, who for the joy that was set before him endured the cross, despising the shame, and is seated at the right hand of the throne of God."

"For the Joy," an odd statement especially when facing a very painful death. As God's son, He gained joy after the pain and shame of the cross because He reconciled us to God. It reminds me of 'blessed are the peacemakers ….'

Ephesians 2:13-16: "But now in Christ Jesus you who once were far off have been brought near by the blood of Christ. For he himself is our peace, who has made us both one and has broken down in his flesh the dividing wall of hostility by abolishing the law of commandments expressed in ordinances, that he might create in himself one new man in place of the two, so making peace, and might reconcile us both to God in one body through the cross, thereby killing the hostility."

On the cross, Jesus reconciled Israel, previously God's chosen nation, with the gentiles, everyone else. Furthermore, He reconciled all mankind to God and the hostility that separated both. All mankind may now choose to be a part of the 'Chosen" nation or Church, not just Israel.

Galatians 3:13-14: "Christ redeemed us from the curse of the law by becoming a curse for us—for it is written, 'Cursed is everyone who is hanged on a tree'—so that in Christ Jesus the blessing of Abraham might come to the Gentiles, so that we might receive the promised Spirit through faith."

The cross removes the impossible standard of the law of Moses. Jesus was the only one to fulfill it without sin. Through Jesus, we become heirs to the promise of Abraham and the indwelling Spirit of God.

Romans 5:8-9: "But God shows his love for us in that while we were still sinners, Christ died for us. Since, therefore, we have now been justified by his blood, much more shall we be saved by him from the wrath of God."

Amazing! Jesus died for us while we were still filthy by sin. His blood saves us from God's wrath. He offered forgiveness or reconciliation before we even asked for what we so desperately needed.

Matthew 10:38: "And whoever does not take his cross and follow me is not worthy of me."

Once we accept His grace by faith, we must pick up our cross and follow Him, live for him, not for our own worldly or sinful desires. Those who refuse to bear their cross do so at their own peril.

Matthew 16:24: "Then Jesus told his disciples, 'If anyone would come after me, let him deny himself and take up his cross and follow me.'"

Follow Him. As opposed to, do as we please.

Mark 8:34: "And calling the crowd to him with his disciples, he said to them, 'If anyone would come after me, let him deny himself and take up his cross and follow me.'"

Becoming a Christian is a gift. But you have to open the gift and use it to "actually receive the gift." A gift unopened is a gift not received. Salvation not accepted and put to use is no salvation at all.

Luke 9:23: "And he said to all, 'If anyone would come after me, let him deny himself and take up his cross daily and follow me.'"

Cross bearing is a daily activity. Church on Sunday is encouraging and a powerful way to worship, but Jesus desires 24/7 cross-carrying. There is no such thing as a part-time disciple, in or out, yes or no. Fence-riding is not allowed.

Jesus died on the cross.

———

The Resurrection Occurred

Matthew 28:5-7: "The angel said to the women, 'Don't be afraid. I know you are looking for Jesus, the one who was killed on the cross. But he is not here. He has risen from death, as he said he would. Come and see the place where his body was. And go quickly and tell his followers, "Jesus has risen from death. He is going into Galilee and will be there before you. You will see him there."' Then the angel said, 'Now I have told you.'"

WOW, now the world has reason to celebrate. "He is not here," an angelic being declares. "He is risen." The angel states and then invites the loyal to look. "Go and tell His followers." With faith and literary license, let's expand. The heavens are declaring the risen Savior to disciples of Jesus and then charging them to do what Jesus will charge all disciples to accomplish. Go. Tell. He is gone, just as He said, but you will see Him later.

Some will see Him on a walk to Emmaus, some in an upper room (doors locked but He is not bound by any earthly barrier), some in Galilee at the seashore when He cooks fish and the disciples give up an occupation to take on a mission. Everything is changed. Death is conquered. Satan's power is diminished and his demise inevitable. Followers become known as Christians. Christians, through faith, become saints. Saints have a home reserved for eternity. The power of death is destroyed for all who believe on the resurrected one. God raised Him. He has the power and authority to raise us. The war is won, and God, Jesus, and the Holy Spirit are victors. Yes, there will be battles and skirmishes for us to fight, but take heart, Jesus has overcome the world. As the song states, "The battle belongs to the Lord."

In the next few pages, we will examine what the resurrection meant then, now, and in the future. We will come to understand how the gospel (good news) is based on the resurrected Christ. We can revel in a life so well lived that it is extended to Jesus's followers as an "eternal" life with him. The resurrection is enough, in that it brings eternal life, but it is much more.

The resurrection occurred.

Resurrection Passages and Commentary

Matthew 16:21: "From that time Jesus began to show his disciples that he must go to Jerusalem and suffer many things from the elders and chief priests and scribes, and be killed, and on the third day be raised."

Near the end of his earthly mission, Jesus began prophesying to His disciples about His impending demise. The four books of the gospels all have such passages. Jesus was becoming more open with the twelve disciples. It seemed that they need to be forewarned repeatedly as they were slow to grasp the reality of Jesus's (God's) plan. In these conversations, Jesus mentioned who, where and what would happen (Matthew 17:22, 23; Mark 8 and 9).

Matthew 27:51-53: "And behold, the curtain of the temple was torn in two, from top to bottom. And the earth shook, and the rocks were split. The tombs also were opened. And many bodies of the saints who had fallen asleep were raised, and coming out of the tombs after his resurrection they went into the holy city and appeared to many."

This passage relates several interesting events after Jesus's death. Note in verse 53 that after His resurrection, many saints returned from the grave or tombs and were seen in Jerusalem. We have no idea how long they were present before returning to the grave, but it appears to be the first evidence of others returning from death because of Jesus's resurrection. (Nice.)

John 11:24-27: "Martha said to him, 'I know that he will rise again in the resurrection on the last day.' Jesus said to her, 'I am the resurrection and the life. Whoever believes in me, though he die, yet shall he live, and everyone who lives and believes in me shall never die. Do you believe this?' She said to him, 'Yes, Lord; I believe that you are the Christ, the Son of God, who is coming into the world.'"

Lazarus, a good friend of Jesus and brother to Mary and Martha, dies. Jesus arrives four days after, and Lazarus is already in the grave. The verses above show the knowledge and faith that Mary had in Jesus. Jesus teaches her that He, the Messiah, is more than a healer. He is "the resurrection and the life." The faithful will die physically but still be resurrected. In fact, believers never "die" in a spiritual sense, but only physically. The human spirit lives on until called by Jesus. This is insight we have today through scripture yet unavailable to most people in Jesus's ministry.

1 Thessalonians 4:13-18: "But we do not want you to be uninformed, brothers, about those who are asleep, that you may not grieve as others do

who have no hope. For since we believe that Jesus died and rose again, even so, through Jesus, God will bring with him those who have fallen asleep. For this we declare to you by a word from the Lord, that we who are alive, who are left until the coming of the Lord, will not precede those who have fallen asleep. For the Lord himself will descend from heaven with a cry of command, with the voice of an archangel, and with the sound of the trumpet of God. And the dead in Christ will rise first. Then we who are alive, who are left, will be caught up together with them in the clouds to meet the Lord in the air, and so we will always be with the Lord. Therefore encourage one another with these words. When Jesus returns to claim his own, the dead will be raised first and those still alive will join them."

Isn't it nice that those who have waited the longest will be first to enter the glory of heaven? Those most recent converts will join them and receive their just reward. "He that is last will be . . ."

1 Corinthians 15:1-8: "Now I would remind you, brothers, of the gospel I preached to you, which you received, in which you stand, and by which you are being saved, if you hold fast to the word I preached to you— unless you believed in vain. For I delivered to you as of first importance what I also received: that Christ died for our sins in accordance with the Scriptures, that he was buried, that he was raised on the third day in accordance with the Scriptures, and that he appeared to Cephas, then to the twelve. Then he appeared to more than five hundred brothers at one time, most of whom are still alive, though some have fallen asleep. Then he appeared to James, then to all the apostles. Last of all, as to one untimely born, he appeared also to me."

Paul writes in these verses the gospel. The death, burial, and resurrection of Jesus cleanses us of our sins. He says this is of first importance. Unless we believe in a Risen Savior, we have no hope of eternal life for ourselves. Paul also reminds them of some five hundred eyewitnesses who saw the resurrected Christ, Paul being the last of that group to see Jesus in person.

There are so many other scriptures that speak of the resurrection, but I will summarize the thoughts or implications for us today.

The resurrection of Jesus;

- Is a fact verified by five hundred eyewitnesses over a period of seven weeks.
- Is proof of God's power over life and death.
- Proves that death always involves sin, but eternal life is from God.

- Demonstrates there is no immortality outside of Jesus.
- Is the gospel.
- Makes Jesus the only founder of a religion that lives and offers life to others.
- Destroys the power of death over mankind when they belong to Jesus.
- Proves Jesus's identity as the Son of God.
- Proves that Satan is not God.
- Allows a man to reign in heaven at the right hand of God.
- Demonstrates a transformed body incorruptible and transcending the laws of science.
- Inspired the dedication and life path of the twelve apostles to face death and never deny this amazing truth.
- Proves that the life and crucifixion of Jesus was an acceptable sacrifice for our sins.
- Completes the eternal plan of YAHWEH to redeem the creation.
- Makes the grave a short-term rental, not a lease to own.
- Completes Jesus's becoming firstborn of the living and the dead.
- Is our hope.
- Is our goal.
- Is our proof.
- Is ours to be, if, we submit to His will and place our faith in Him who rose.

To be continued . . .

Summary of Chapter 3

Jesus is God.

He was there from before the beginning, and all was made with Him in mind. He is the part of the Trinity that takes on flesh and experienced life much as we do. This makes Him unique in many ways: God, man, Spirit, flesh, firstborn of all creation, and child of Mary. He walks, talks, feels, smells, and hears as a Creator and creation. Jesus is the image of God in the form of man, just as Genesis 2 explains.

His role in eternity is enormous: Creator, sustainer, mediator, Savior, Lord, and servant; a lion and a lamb; able to defeat Satan in the wilderness and the grave. And yet a sinless sacrifice for our sin; the perfect example, adored by most who meet Him and get to know Him; a healer, teacher, and friend to people. Lastly an accuser, judge, and threat to hypocrites, false teachers, and the ungodly.

His return will condemn most people. All who have not bent the knee and confessed His name will do so *after* it is too late. His return will be praised and glorified by all who chose and, by faith, bowed and confessed Him before fleshly death. They will hear words like "Well done, my good and faithful servant." They will be invited home to reign with Jesus.

Jesus is God.

CHAPTER FOUR

The Holy Spirit

The Holy Spirit is God. How do you write about the Holy Spirit? As God, the third part of the Trinity, the Holy Spirit is God at work on earth. Again, as in previous sections, we see the Holy Spirit as God in His third part. Steam, liquid, and ice are just different ways to experience water. God the Father, Son, and Holy Spirit are three ways He reveals Himself.

In Genesis, the Holy Spirit makes itself known while hovering over the waters doing the works of creation. As Yahweh and Jesus are presented as male, so is the Holy Spirit in many instances. One major difference, though, is in some instances, the word chosen for the Holy Spirit in the Greek language can be feminine or neutral. Not being a Greek or Hebrew scholar, this author depends on supposedly knowledgeable individuals & the Holy Spirit for answers. Listening for hidden or overt agendas, most, like myself, allow the scripture to define or translate itself. As such, it appears that the Holy Spirit is seen most often in the male persona but with many uses of female attributes or characteristics. Some languages also on some occasions see it as gender-neutral. Throughout this study, I will use "He," "Spirit," "Spirit of God," and "Holy Spirit" interchangeably and allow you to do your own study if it helps in understanding. When speaking of the human spirit, I will not capitalize the "s" or "h."

The Spirit is the God of action on earth. From creation through the thousands of years mankind experiences on earth, until Christ comes again, the Holy Spirit is on earth doing the will of God. The Spirit comes "upon" people in the Old Testament in multiple examples. In the New Testament, this same Spirit indwells or fills the saved as well as performs miracles and a host of other activities. People and scripture portray the Spirit as a miracle worker, carrying the load, ever-present, busy, comforter, counselor, and many other characteristics and activities. With complete unity of mind and purpose, this God spends most of our time calling us to salvation through the scripture, wording our prayers to the Father, responding to our need for guidance, as well as being our seal of redemption.

In the pages that follow, many examples of His work will be presented from both the Old and New testament. To keep this book concise, not every act or characteristic will be detailed. Hopefully, after reading this section, your hunger to learn more will lead you in a more comprehensive study. And away we go!

The Holy Spirit is God.

Holy Spirit as Creator

Genesis 1:1-2 "In the beginning, God created the heavens and the earth. The earth was without form and void, and darkness was over the face of the deep. And the Spirit of God was hovering over the face of the waters."

As with Father God and Jesus, the Holy Spirit is present in the creation. The scripture reads that as a Spirit, He hovers above the water. That places Him in direct proximity to where the action will be happening. He is not taking on fleshly form or solid shape, for He is not only totally Spirit, third part of a whole, but holy as well. Be amazed! An invisible, all-powerful, ever-present holiness chooses to be a part of creation and places itself right in the midst of the process.

In Psalms 33:6-7 the writer tells us, "By the word of the Lord the heavens were made, and by the breath of his mouth all their host. He gathers the waters of the sea as a heap; he puts the deeps in storehouses."

In this reading, God's breath is a part of creating all the angels, cherubim, and seraphim. Any and all creatures that have or currently reside in heaven are credited to the Holy Spirit's movement. In the book of Job, Elihu, a young man who has listened to Job and his three friends debate Job's losses, condition, and the possibility of Job's misery being the consequence of sin, now wants to speak. He is young and has waited for the older men to finish. In Job 33:4 "The Spirit of God has made me, and the breath of the Almighty gives me life."

It becomes evident that the Holy Spirit was more than present at creation but is also a Creator. From these and other verses in scripture, we can be assured that the Holy Spirit is also Creator as is the Father and Son.

The Holy Spirit is Creator.

THE HOLY SPIRIT WORKS IN THE OLD TESTAMENT

Psalms 51 and Isaiah 63 are the only two chapters in the Jewish Bible (commonly known as the Old Testament) that use the words "Holy" and "Spirit" next to each other.

Psalm 51:11 "Cast me not away from your presence, and take not your Holy Spirit from me."

Psalms 51, verses 1-12, is a plea for forgiveness. The writer is acknowledging his sins and asking God to cleanse him. He confesses his sin is against God (all sin is against God as He is the moral-setter and law-giver). He expresses a concern that God might discard him from His presence or even remove His Holy Spirit from him. It reads like pleading, a heartfelt petition more than a simple request. Removal of the Holy Spirit is the ultimate rejection for a God-seeker. When speaking of any person seeking to please God, being rejected by the Holy Spirit, or turning away from the Spirit of God without repentance and forgiveness, leads to eternal death of body and soul. David, the greatest king of Israel, was a God-seeker. Twice called a man "after God's own heart" (1 Samuel 13:14, Acts 13:22), he was imploring God to forgive his sin.

Continuing this psalm, David states he will teach others not to sin. He will sing of God's righteousness and declare his praise. He shares an insight: God loves a humble, contrite heart more than blood sacrifices of animals. With the knowledge provided by the Holy Spirit, he knows God looks more on the inside of people than the outward appearance. Our intent is taken into consideration as well as our behavior.

The second place we see the words "Holy Spirit" adjoined in the Old Testament is in Isaiah.

Isaiah 63:10-14 "But they rebelled and grieved his Holy Spirit; therefore he turned to be their enemy, and himself fought against them. Then he remembered the days of old, of Moses and his people. Where is he who brought them up out of the sea with the shepherds of his flock? Where is he who put in the midst of them his Holy Spirit, who caused his glorious arm to go at the right hand of Moses, who divided the waters before them to make for himself an everlasting name, who led them through the depths? Like a horse in the desert, they did not stumble. Like livestock that go down into the valley, the Spirit of the Lord gave them rest. So you led your people, to make for yourself a glorious name."

Other English translations may have more or less occurrences where these words are joined as a name or identifier, but most often Spirit of God or God's Spirit is the name used in Genesis through Malachi.

In chapter 63, the prophet Isaiah is nearing the end of the messages God told him to relate to the nation of Israel. The first six verses appear to be about Yahweh and His execution of wrath on sinners. Verses 7-9 tell of days past where God had showered love, compassion, and blessings upon the twelve tribes of Israel. Verses 10-14 recount their rebellion and how they grieved His Holy Spirit. In memory, mention of God's previous deeds of saving Israel from bondage are summarized. The conclusion of chapter 63 is a desire for God to return and save them as if He was the one who rejected them first. He did not.

Is it not interesting that the only two times we find this wording, "Holy Spirit," in the Old Testament is also when the Spirit is being grieved or a fear of His removal? It is hoped that later in the New Testament, this grieving or removal will take on a new deeper meaning.

The Holy Spirit is in the Old Testament.

THE SPIRIT OF GOD CAN BE "SENSED"

Genesis 41:38-40: "And Pharaoh said to his servants, 'Can we find a man like this, in whom is the Spirit of God?' Then Pharaoh said to Joseph, 'Since God has shown you all this, there is none so discerning and wise as you are. You shall be over my house, and all my people shall order themselves as you command. Only as regards the throne will I be greater than you.'"

A little history, Joseph, sold into slavery by his brothers, has full faith in God. In one position after another, Joseph, by God's desire, succeeds and is eventually brought to the pharaoh's attention to repeat and interpret a dream. Joseph, in prison at that time, is cleaned up and presented to court. He is able to meet the challenge required of him and is rewarded for doing so. The pharaoh is extremely impressed, and he gives this former prisoner the equivalent of a prime minister's position. Notice that in verse 38, the pharaoh gives credit to Joseph as a man with the "Spirit of God" in him.

No one had to tell him how the prophesy was given. Joseph did not bill himself as a man of God, sorcerer, or prophet. But the pharaoh could tell because no one could do what had been done without the Spirit of God. The Holy Spirit occasionally reveals Himself to others through miracles, God's people, as well as the word. Let us look at another example.

Daniel 4:4-9: "I, Nebuchadnezzar, was at ease in my house and prospering in my palace. I saw a dream that made me afraid. As I lay in bed the fancies and the visions of my head alarmed me. So I made a decree that all the wise men of Babylon should be brought before me, that they might make known to me the interpretation of the dream. Then the magicians, the enchanters, the Chaldeans, and the astrologers came in, and I told them the dream, but they could not make known to me its interpretation. At last Daniel came in before me—he who was named Belteshazzar after the name of my god, and in whom is the spirit of the holy gods—and I told him the dream, saying, 'O Belteshazzar, chief of the magicians, because I know that the spirit of the holy gods is in you and that no mystery is too difficult for you, tell me the visions of my dream that I saw and their interpretation.'"

The background of this encounter starts with Babylon conquering Judah, the last Israelite nation, and taking the best and brightest back to Babylon. Daniel is renamed, assimilated, and educated in the Babylonian culture to work for Babylon. King Nebuchadnezzar has a dream (chapter

2) that only God could interpret. Daniel is given the interpretation and shares it with the king. The king is dazzled and promoted Daniel and his three (Israelite) friends to high positions in Babylon. He also gave homage to Daniel and praise to God.

So in chapter 4, there is another dream no one can interpret. Daniel is called in to the palace, and again, God gives him the interpretation. This time is somewhat different as the king states his knowledge that Daniel has the "spirit of the gods" in him. Let us forgive King Nebuchadnezzar for not using God's name or for believing there are multiple gods. He is a pagan. But even non-believers can recognize the Spirit of God at work in situations where there are no other explanations.

The Holy Spirit can be "sensed".

The Holy Spirit Enables the Chosen

Of the many activities the Holy Spirit performs, imparting skills, knowledge, and abilities above and beyond the natural, is one of the most frequent we see in the Old and New Testaments. Read the following passage from Exodus:

Exodus 35:30-35: "Then Moses said to the people of Israel, 'See, the Lord has called by name Bezalel the son of Uri, son of Hur, of the tribe of Judah; and he has filled him with the Spirit of God, with skill, with intelligence, with knowledge, and with all craftsmanship, to devise artistic designs, to work in gold and silver and bronze, in cutting stones for setting, and in carving wood, for work in every skilled craft. And he has inspired him to teach, both him and Oholiab the son of Ahisamach of the tribe of Dan. He has filled them with skill to do every sort of work done by an engraver or by a designer or by an embroiderer in blue and purple and scarlet yarns and fine twined linen, or by a weaver—by any sort of workman or skilled designer.'"

In Ex. 31, the LORD tells Moses that God has gifted Bezalel and others for artistic work. They are to design and build the holy tabernacle God will inhabit during the wilderness journey. This "tent of meeting" will house many articles, including the Ark of the Covenant, Aaron's staff, gold artifacts, and censers. The holy place, the most holy place, and altar are just a few of the worship areas included in and near the tabernacle. In this reading, Moses shares this information with the people of Israel. Imagine being gifted by the Spirit of God to develop such a dwelling for God. What an honor!

In Matthew 10:16-20, Jesus informs His disciples that they will be handed over to authorities and questioned: "Behold, I am sending you out as sheep in the midst of wolves, so be wise as serpents and innocent as doves. Beware of men, for they will deliver you over to courts and flog you in their synagogues, and you will be dragged before governors and kings for my sake, to bear witness before them and the Gentiles. When they deliver you over, do not be anxious how you are to speak or what you are to say, for what you are to say will be given to you in that hour. For it is not you who speak, but the Spirit of your Father speaking through you."

This promise given to the twelve disciples is one I have claimed/ requested on several occasions often when teaching or in a Bible study where it is particularly important that I say the right word, the right way. I remind God (silent prayer) of this promise, and He has never failed me. On the other hand, when I answer on my own, I have sometimes struggled or, worse, hastened or allowed my ego to lead my mouth. I am not nearly as effective as the Spirit.

The Spirit of God can enable the chosen.

THE SPIRIT OF GOD GIVES GOD'S MESSAGE TO HIS PROPHETS

The role of a prophet in the Old Testament differs from the role of a priest. The two major activities of a prophet are to preach God's message and, occasionally, to foretell future events; whereas a priest offers sacrifices to atone for people's sins and acts as a mediator between the people and God. So a prophet stands to share God's message to the follower, while the priest facilitates worship/forgiveness between the people and God. In the following readings, we see a prophet telling of a future event.

Isaiah 61:1-3: "The Spirit of the Lord God is upon me, because the Lord has anointed me to bring good news to the poor; he has sent me to bind up the brokenhearted, to proclaim liberty to the captives, and the opening of the prison to those who are bound; to proclaim the year of the Lord's favor, and the day of vengeance of our God; to comfort all who mourn; to grant to those who mourn in Zion—to give them a beautiful headdress instead of ashes, the oil of gladness instead of mourning, the garment of praise instead of a faint spirit; that they may be called oaks of righteousness, the planting of the Lord, that he may be glorified."

These verses are a small portion of a prophesy foretelling the Messiah's (Jesus) future coming. Notice how the "Spirit" is upon Isaiah. It is the words of God given to this prophet, who is to share it with the people. There are many instances in both covenants where the Spirit facilitates similar messages from God. Paul, an apostle for Jesus, had the following encounter.

Acts 21:10-11: "While we were staying for many days, a prophet named Agabus came down from Judea. And coming to us, he took Paul's belt and bound his own feet and hands and said, 'Thus says the Holy Spirit, "This is how the Jews at Jerusalem will bind the man who owns this belt and deliver him into the hands of the Gentiles."'"

If you continue reading, Paul is not dissuaded by this prophesy and continues on toward Jerusalem. Shortly afterward, the prophesy comes true, and Paul is eventually tried in Rome because of his and Jesus's Jewish enemies.

The Spirit gives the prophet the words of God.

THE SPIRIT OF GOD CAN APPEAR VISUALLY

Most people of the "book" know God is a Spirit and that Jesus was a Spirit who took on flesh. So obviously, the Holy Spirit is also invisible yet present. However, people often do not understand that the Holy Spirit can appear in a visual form. The next passage concerns Jesus's baptism.

Matthew 3:13-17: "Then Jesus came from Galilee to the Jordan to John, to be baptized by him. John would have prevented him, saying, 'I need to be baptized by you, and do you come to me?' But Jesus answered him, 'Let it be so now, for thus it is fitting for us to fulfill all righteousness.' Then he consented. And when Jesus was baptized, immediately he went up from the water, and behold, the heavens were opened to him, and he saw the Spirit of God descending like a dove and coming to rest on him; and behold, a voice from heaven said, 'This is my beloved Son, with whom I am well pleased.'"

Jesus desires water baptism. John (the Baptist) wants Jesus to baptize him, but Jesus explains they are fulfilling all righteousness. The heavens opened, and the Holy Spirit appears as a dove and lands on Jesus. Pretty amazing event. God tells the witnesses who Jesus is and that He loves him and approves of Him. There is much more theology that we could discuss from this, but that is not the purpose of this writing. The point is that the Spirit can and does take on an appearance when He desires.

In another section, we see the Holy Spirit as "tongues of fire."

Acts 2:1-4: "When the day of Pentecost arrived, they were all together in one place. And suddenly there came from heaven a sound like a mighty rushing wind, and it filled the entire house where they were sitting. And divided tongues as of fire appeared to them and rested on each one of them. And they were all filled with the Holy Spirit and began to speak in other tongues as the Spirit gave them utterance."

This passage refers to the twelve apostles receiving the Holy Spirit after Jesus's ascension to heaven. Jesus had told them to return to Jerusalem to await this anointing. Upon receiving the Spirit of God, they were able to speak in various languages. Reading further in this chapter, we find Peter preaching to a crowd from twelve countries. He and the other apostles were able to be understood in each listener's native language.

The Holy Spirit can take on visual appearances.

The Spirit Is Our Prayer Partner and Petitioner

Speaking personally, the Holy Spirit's involvement in my prayers and growth are sincerely appreciated. In fact, they are coveted. Prayer minus the Holy Spirit wastes breath and the opportunity to commune with Yahweh. As kids, many of us learned to "pray" for meals, before bed, and when punishment was imminent. Growing up and achieving the ability to think more abstractly presents us with a spiritual understanding of prayer beyond "please" and "thank you." Once we receive the indwelling of the Holy Spirit, amazing things happen.

Romans 8:26-28: "Likewise the Spirit helps us in our weakness. For we do not know what to pray for as we ought, but the Spirit himself intercedes for us with groanings too deep for words. And he who searches hearts knows what the mind of the Spirit is, because the Spirit intercedes for the saints according to the will of God. And we know that for those who love God all things work together for good, for those who are called according to his purpose."

The apostle Paul, writing to a Roman Christian church, explains some of the deeper workings of the Spirit of God. It interprets our thoughts/ requests as a translator might translate English into French. This analogy is not entirely accurate but provides a metaphor for "God-speak." Maybe when the perfect comes (heaven), the saved will be able to speak in this manner also. Beyond this, Paul also states that the Spirit intercedes for us as God wills, explaining more fully how God often interacts and orchestrates the mega-ka-zillion (made up word of infinite zeroes) things He does. This is not a promise of lifting more weight, running faster, etc. It is about his purpose, not ours.

Jesus speaks to some of the Holy Spirit actions in John 14:25-26: "These things I have spoken to you while I am still with you. But the Helper, the Holy Spirit, whom the Father will send in my name, he will teach you all things and bring to your remembrance all that I have said to you."

Jesus was speaking to the twelve disciples, but in a way, it applies to us. Those who read and study scripture, especially the New Testament, find passages coming into memory when we need a reminder or when praying for God's promises.

The Holy Spirit is our prayer partner and petitioner.

THE HOLY SPIRIT IS A TEACHER
AND REMINDER

One of the things Jesus never worried about was how to teach the disciples in such a manner that they would remember everything when preaching or repeating the gospel. He knows our limitation and distractions. He knows we are living in a fallen world. He knows we do not all learn the same way. So rather than risk His message being inadvertently misstated, He promised the Holy Spirit. Listen to the apostle John as he writes, "These things I have spoken to you while I am still with you. But the Helper, the Holy Spirit, whom the Father will send in my name, he will teach you all things and bring to your remembrance all that I have said to you" (John 14:25-26).

At this point in Jesus's life, He is preparing His followers, especially the twelve apostles, for His own departure and their mission. Much of chapter 14 concerns the Holy Spirit being sent by the Father, how God and Jesus would make Their home with Christians (indwelling), and how God's Spirit would be a comfort to them.

Today people who do not know scripture, God, or how to live a life of love find it even harder to understand "God in us." Often, when people receive the Spirit, there is no special "a-ha." Rather, for most, it is a gentle awakening as they begin the life they have chosen. As they listen to fellow believers, read scripture, pray, and seek guidance, the Holy Spirit makes itself known. Many people experience the Spirit first through prayer or song, but as they grow in Christ and open themselves to communion with God, the Spirit becomes more familiar and active. In fact, the only "Christians" who deny an active Spirit are those who want to limit Him (or have been taught He is limited to indwelling and/or prayer interpretation) from acting in His role as God. It seems as if people only equate an active Holy Spirit with the miraculous deeds of Jesus and the first century. Those supernatural events were to convince viewers and us of the fact that Jesus was the Son of God. The Holy Spirit was incredibly involved in those events as He is now involved in our day-to-day lives.

Many a time preachers and teachers rely on the Spirit to ensure the right words are used and spoken in the right way. Relying on the Spirit to find passages, topics, or express specific thoughts is a time-honored approach to developing a lesson. Many hours of prayer enlisting the Spirit's help are spent by saints everywhere. And He delivers, often in amazing, unimagined ways that leave the disciple shocked and with the certain knowledge that it came from God. It could only have come from God. The Holy Spirit's participation in Christian lives is only limited by our denial or refusal to accept and seek its intervention by faith.

Two other passages to support this teaching: The first is from Mark 13:9-11: "But be on your guard. For they will deliver you over to councils, and you will be beaten in synagogues, and you will stand before governors and kings for my sake, to bear witness before them. And the gospel must first be proclaimed to all nations. And when they bring you to trial and deliver you over, do not be anxious beforehand what you are to say, but say whatever is given you in that hour, for it is not you who speak, but the Holy Spirit."

Here, the Spirit will give the listeners the words to speak when questioned by the authorities. This is just one method of teaching to prepare them for future events or to learn the important things God wishes to reveal to this audience. A second passage comes from John.

1 John 2:26, 27: "I write these things to you about those who are trying to deceive you. 27 But the anointing that you received from him abides in you, and you have no need that anyone should teach you. But as his anointing teaches you about everything, and is true, and is no lie—just as it has taught you, abide in him."

This narrative gives mature Christians encouragement and strength, when they are presented with a false teaching. In essence, the Holy Spirit has taught them, and He resides in them, so do not be deceived. To receive the Spirit of God, one must confess Jesus as God's Son, your Savior, and accept Him as Lord of your life. This is a part of the salvation process that allows God to send the indwelling Spirit.

The Holy Spirit is a teacher and reminder.

The Holy Spirit Is a Guide for Our Walk

From birth until death, we all are on a path. That path or journey involves all the experiences of life. There are many choices to be made, and each has a consequence. "Consequence" is a neutral word that means outcome. Outcomes or consequences can be natural or artificial/imposed. Regardless, they are authored by the choice made.

An example of a natural consequence can be seen in the act of driving too fast. Natural consequences include arriving sooner, less time on the road; for some, it raises excitement and for others, causes fear. In the extreme, a collision with injuries and death is possible. An artificial or imposed consequence might include being pulled over by the police. This might result in a ticket and fine, increased insurance rates, losing your license to drive, or negatively making an impact on your reputation.

From this example, it becomes obvious that consequences follow choices and action. Generally lawful, helpful, compassionate, and high moral choices lead to favorable consequences. The less-desired consequences generally follow selfish, deceitful, harmful, or immoral decisions, the choice that is acted upon being the catalyst. Scripture repeatedly teaches, explains, demonstrates, and admonishes us to make loving, compassionate, and Spirit-led decisions and actions. The opposite of Spirit-led is fleshly-directed decision-making. Fleshly-steered choices are lust-of-the-eye, lust-of-the-flesh, and pride-of-life (ego)-guided. Read the following scripture.

Galatians 5:16-21: "But I say, walk by the Spirit, and you will not gratify the desires of the flesh. For the desires of the flesh are against the Spirit, and the desires of the Spirit are against the flesh, for these are opposed to each other, to keep you from doing the things you want to do. But if you are led by the Spirit, you are not under the law. Now the works of the flesh are evident: sexual immorality, impurity, sensuality, idolatry, sorcery, enmity, strife, jealousy, fits of anger, rivalries, dissensions, divisions, envy, drunkenness, orgies, and things like these. I warn you, as I warned you before, that those who do such things will not inherit the kingdom of God."

The writer of Galatians is Paul, an apostle of God, inspired by the Holy Spirit to warn this church of following fleshly or sinful desires. He gives many examples in verses 19-21 and warns that those who live in like manner will not inherit heaven. He even added "that those who do such things," suggesting there are other harmful acts not listed. The sum of scripture explains how people who have previously lived this way or Christians who occasionally sin, now can be forgiven. Either way, to not live this way avoids the natural or imposed consequences that so commonly plague society. No drunkenness (safe homes, work, and highways) fits of anger, (words spoken that hurt or assaults), sexual immorality (unwanted pregnancies, broken marriages, and kids without a parent), and the list goes on. Every fleshly behavior on the list makes an impact to at least one other person. All sin is against God, and yet those closest to the sinner also are affected. Reading on, we see how the Spirit can offer a healthy way of life.

Galatians 5:22-24: "But the fruit of the Spirit is love, joy, peace, patience, kindness, goodness, faithfulness, gentleness, self-control; against such things there is no law. And those who belong to Christ Jesus have crucified the flesh with its passions and desires.

People who choose to live in the Spirit generally enjoy a more comfortable life. The "fruits" comes from making spiritual choices and acting upon them. Love is an action, not an emotion. Love is demonstrated, not withheld. Joy is a gift that exceeds happiness. Peace makes it easy to sleep and ensures more gracious interaction with others. Kindness is selfless and makes it easy to share with others. Goodness becomes a trait that others can depend on, knowing who and what you are. Faithfulness establishes your level of integrity to others and enhances your witness. Gentleness draws the hurting to you for aid and comfort. Self-control keeps us from rash actions and decisions. Self-control sets an example for the young and immature to aspire for themselves. It also eliminates the need for "other control," jail, handcuffs, etc.

And as stated, there is no law, government, authority, king, or administrator that does not want their followers to demonstrate these qualities. This is the stuff that employers seek and so often cannot find. This is the kind of child all parents would dream to raise, and the best of parents want to live in this manner.

The Holy Spirit is a guide for our walk.

The Holy Spirit Grants Courage

Ever been scared? Not just startled or anxious, but truly terrified—knees weak, sweating, pale, and panic-filled? Soldiers in battle can explain it to you better than this writer. There are times in life, hopefully very few, when the only logical response is to be petrified. Christians are no different than others when confronting an overwhelming threat. Facing a prejudiced authority when innocence can make one scared, especially when you are innocent, and yet the judge is biased and looking for some way to nail you. This was the case when Peter and John were arrested for—get this—healing a crippled man. Acts 4 tells the story. The Jewish high priest arrested, held overnight, held an interrogation the next day for the two apostles, two uneducated guys facing the ruling power of the Jewish nation. When questioned by what authority (power) they had healed this man, notice what the Bible says:

Acts 4:8-10: "Then Peter, filled with the Holy Spirit, said to them, 'Rulers of the people and elders, if we are being examined today concerning a good deed done to a crippled man, by what means this man has been healed, let it be known to all of you and to all the people of Israel that by the name of Jesus Christ of Nazareth, whom you crucified, whom God raised from the dead—by him this man is standing before you well."

The Holy Spirit-filled Peter responded with clarity and boldness. Also, notice in verse 10 that he reminded them that they (the Jewish rulers) had crucified Jesus. Notice that these two Apostles are correcting the Sanhedrin Court when, by all reasoning, should be looking for a way out of trouble. Instead were boldly telling the truth and reminding them of their sin. This was not what the high priest wanted said, especially in front of many witnesses. So trying to save face and keep from making matters worse, they went into a private session. Looking for a way to squelch the apostles and yet not anger the crowd, they insisted Peter and John hush up about Jesus. Peter, again, very brashly replied that if it was a choice of obeying God or them, they would obey God. After some more threats were made, the priest released them.

The two found their friends, told the story, and everyone praised God. Later they prayed. Notice the request they made in that prayer:

Acts 4:29-31: "And now, Lord, look upon their threats and grant to your servants to continue to speak your word with all boldness, while you stretch out your hand to heal, and signs and wonders are performed through the name of your holy servant Jesus.' And when they had prayed, the place in which they were gathered together was shaken, and they were all filled with the Holy Spirit and continued to speak the word of God with boldness."

When empowered by the Holy Spirit, Christians can do what is needed with confidence. Examples abound in scripture and in life. In many countries, Christianity is illegal or forbidden by the government. Yet year after year, missionaries and local believers continue to teach the gospel under fear of imprisonment, torture, and death. Why? They are saved (have the indwelling of the Holy Spirit) and want others to have the same opportunity. They risk freedom, reputation, shunning, and other harmful consequences to bring the good news of Jesus to a lost nation or people.

The Holy Spirit grants courage.

THE HOLY SPIRIT IS THE
SEAL OF REDEMPTION

Back in the day, a seal on an official document authenticated the letter to be from the original source. The king, businessman, or noblemen would have a stamp or ring engraved specifically for their use. When dipped in ink or pressed in hot wax, then stamped or sealed, it was verification of originality. Today seals come in all manner of material, sometimes applied to show the container is unopened, and thus, the contents are the original items sent. Another reason to seal might be to prove a door has not been opened since the seal was applied. Regardless, the original reason remains unchanged. The seal proves the contents to be authentic and undeniable as to ownership or authority. The Holy Spirit is the seal of redemption. In Ephesians, the apostle Paul writes the following message:

Ephesians 1:13-14: "In him you also, when you heard the word of truth, the gospel of your salvation, and believed in him, were sealed with the promised Holy Spirit, who is the guarantee of our inheritance until we acquire possession of it, to the praise of his glory."

Our belief or faith in Jesus is rewarded now by being sealed by the Holy Spirit. The Spirit of God identifies the saved and guarantees their salvation until they arrive in heaven. In this moment, God concludes the adoption of the saints by bringing us home. Having volunteered and worked as a Court-Appointed Special Advocate (CASA) in several adoption proceedings, I have seen this firsthand. Selecting a child, the trial, and supervised placements are not an adoption. Court approval and changing the child's surname to yours is not the adoption. The adoption is complete when the new parent/s take the child home and personally assumes responsibility for loving, training, and ensuring the well-being of the child. The only difference between God and mankind's adoption is that we have already been trained to trust our "Father" completely. Our adoption will be complete after Jesus presents his Church to God.

It is believed that Apostle Paul wrote three or possibly four letters to the church at Corinth. Two of these "epistles" are included in the New Testament. In the quote below, Paul explains how that church and these who brought the gospel to Corinth are sealed in the same way by the Holy Spirit.

2 Corinthians 1:20-22: "For all the promises of God find their Yes in him. That is why it is through him that we utter our Amen to God for his glory. And it is God who establishes us with you in Christ, and has anointed us, and who has also put his seal on us and given us his Spirit in our hearts as a guarantee."

The assembly (people, not building) of Christians can be described as those authenticated by Jesus to enter the kingdom of God. This is what we call the church of Christ. It is not a denominational name but a spiritual collection of all the saved (sealed in Christ) worldwide, regardless of the century they lived or place they worshipped, praised, and communed with Christ. This seal should increase our confidence and strengthen our faith in the one who died for us.

Later in the same book, Paul uses the metaphor of a tent versus dwelling with God. Ponder the following paragraph:

2 Corinthians 5:1-5: "For we know that if the tent that is our earthly home is destroyed, we have a building from God, a house not made with hands, eternal in the heavens. For in this tent we groan, longing to put on our heavenly dwelling, if indeed by putting it on we may not be found naked. For while we are still in this tent, we groan, being burdened—not that we would be unclothed, but that we would be further clothed, so that what is mortal may be swallowed up by life. He who has prepared us for this very thing is God, who has given us the Spirit as a guarantee."

His reference of naked can be taken as vulnerable. On this earth, there is a sense of insecurity or vulnerability that will not be present in heaven. Even if Covid-19 or threats of war may deprive us of physical peace, Christians enjoy spiritual peace. With the Spirit as the guarantee of eternal life and with the faith people put in this promise, Christians are not naked but will be further clothed once home with God.

Romans 8 has much to say about salvation. The following verses are just a portion of the chapter. Romans 8:9-11: "You, however, are not in the flesh but in the Spirit, if in fact the Spirit of God dwells in you. Anyone who does not have the Spirit of Christ does not belong to him. But if Christ is in you, although the body is dead because of sin, the Spirit is life because of righteousness. If the Spirit of him who raised Jesus from the dead dwells in you, he who raised Christ Jesus from the dead will also give life to your mortal bodies through his Spirit who dwells in you."

One more promise to encourage His disciples. One more piece of scriptural evidence of God's love for His people. One more assurance that our past lives are forgotten and replaced by spiritual influence to live in the Spirit and not in the "world."

The Holy Spirit is the seal of redemption.

To Blaspheme the Holy Spirit Is Deadly

The last topic on the Holy Spirit is sobering. As the Holy Spirit of God serves as a seal for the saved, blaspheming the Spirit of God is an unpardonable (unforgiveable) sin. Sin never forgiven leads to judgment and second death.

John Piper defines blasphemy against the Holy Spirit as "The unforgivable sin of blasphemy against the Holy Spirit is an act of resistance which belittles the Holy Spirit so grievously that he withdraws forever with his convicting power so that we are never able to repent and be forgiven."

In Matthew 12:31-32, Jesus is quoted as saying, "Therefore I tell you, every sin and blasphemy will be forgiven people, but the blasphemy against the Spirit will not be forgiven. And whoever speaks a word against the Son of Man will be forgiven, but whoever speaks against the Holy Spirit will not be forgiven, either in this age or in the age to come."

This statement comes at the end of a passage where Jesus's enemies accuse Jesus of casting out demons by the power of Beelzebub or Satan. Jesus explains very simply how and why they are wrong. He finishes His discourse by saying that you can blaspheme Him and He will forgive you. Not so when you blaspheme the Spirit of God. No demon ever cast out another demon. Jesus cast out the demons through the power of the Holy Spirit (Mt. 12:28). To give Satan credit for God's work is blasphemy and unforgiveable.

So then some might ask, is this the same as quenching or grieving the Spirit of God? Grieving the Spirit can and is forgiven when the guilty party becomes sincerely sorry and penitent of this sin. Historically, as well as today, God forgives the penitent heart after asking for forgiveness. He urges us to forgive as often as necessary.

Matthew 18:21-22: "Then Peter came up and said to him, 'Lord, how often will my brother sin against me, and I forgive him? As many as seven times?' Jesus said to him, 'I do not say to you seven times, but seventy-seven times.'"

Many things grieve the Holy Spirit. Some examples are our sin, ignoring the word, treating people badly, lying, and the list goes on. But quenching of the Spirit is not terminal unless we totally reject the Spirit and once more live in the flesh, turning our back on the gift of salvation.

This total rejection is a form of blasphemy. Consider the following passage from Peter:

2 Peter 2:20-22: "For if, after they have escaped the defilements of the world through the knowledge of our Lord and Savior Jesus Christ, they are again entangled in them and overcome, the last state has become worse for them than the first. For it would have been better for them never to have known the way of righteousness than after knowing it to turn back from the holy commandment delivered to them. What the true proverb says has happened to them: 'The dog returns to its own vomit, and the sow, after washing herself, returns to wallow in the mire.'"

This passage gives an example of someone who became aware of the way of righteousness but later rejected it. Now it does not say they will go to hell, but the inference is that they would be better off to have never known Jesus than to turn their back on righteousness. One gets the sense that this action puts them back in the unrighteous or unsaved life. Dwell on this passage and read all of 2 Peter 2 to see if you come to the same conclusion.

Paul, in his letter to the Ephesians, enlightens Christians on things to avoid and to do in their new life. Slowly read and reflect on the following verses:

Ephesians 4:28-31: "Let the thief no longer steal, but rather let him labor, doing honest work with his own hands, so that he may have something to share with anyone in need. Let no corrupting talk come out of your mouths, but only such as is good for building up, as fits the occasion, that it may give grace to those who hear. And do not grieve the Holy Spirit of God, by whom you were sealed for the day of redemption. Let all bitterness and wrath and anger and clamor and slander be put away from you, along with all malice. Be kind to one another, tenderhearted, forgiving one another, as God in Christ forgave you."

People living as he suggests will not grieve or blaspheme the Holy Spirit to their own demise. Just the opposite, they will grow in relationship, favor, and worth to the church and its founder Jesus.

To blaspheme the Holy Spirit is deadly.

Holy Spirit Summary

As the third part of God, the role of the Spirit is unique and yet amazingly important in the Trinity. As God and Creator, He was involved before creation and was an active force in making the world, from the core of Earth to the furthest points of the galaxy. Still active today, the Spirit of God and Jesus is living within all Christians, acting in many capacities. His impact on the more righteous bears witness to the Spirit's existence and impact on people's lives.

In times past, He has appeared in the form of a dove, tongues of fire, and been heard as the voice of a donkey. The Holy Spirit enhances the abilities of those chosen to carry out Godly tasks. He enables the disciples to speak truth when questioned by authorities and enables the scripture writer to be accurate and truthful in leaving us the words of God.

Often the Holy Spirit gave the prophets of old messages to share with the people. He is our partner in prayer, translating our desires and praise to the Father in language we do not know or understand. From these requests God/ Jesus/ Holy Spirit often enable miracles and answers to occur. The Holy Spirit shares our thoughts with God, He also shares God's word with us. The Spirit teaches, guides, and reminds us of scripture, lessons, and our identity.

As the Bible was written by men inspired by the Holy Spirit, it becomes a guide for those who believe that Father God, Jesus, and the Spirit love us and want us to submit our will to Him; to be selfless instead of selfish, to serve others and to accept service from others, to love our neighbors as ourselves, and to love the assembly in a sacrificial manner.

The Holy Spirit grants courage to those who walk the walk of Jesus, the courage to speak even in the face of persecution, the ability to go on when others ridicule or defame a good person's name.

As the Spirit grants courage, He also teaches wisdom to those who request it. Wisdom and knowledge are especially important in applying God's lessons to the daily walk of mankind. Wisdom is using knowledge appropriately in the situation being faced. An experienced horseman can estimate the age of a horse by looking at its teeth and gums, but to look in the mouth of a "gift" horse in not wise. In fact, it would be insulting to the giver if the receiver were to act in that manner. The wise thing to do would be to accept the gift as given. The result is a strengthened relationship as opposed to being insolent and demeaning the relationship.

Most importantly, the Holy Spirit is granted by Father God and Jesus as a seal or pledge of salvation. What a gift! We are a temple! As a temple, we open ourselves to host the Holy Spirit and be recognized as part of the church, the assembly of Jesus's own while here on earth and a promise of eternal life when the kingdom of God is called home. Think of it this way: As Christians strive to grow in righteousness daily, the Holy One dwells within, assisting them in their efforts. This is why it is so important to remember never to blaspheme the Holy Spirit. Be careful not to grieve the Spirit as sometimes this 'living in the flesh' can become habitual and lead to the denial of the Spirit and eternal death.

CHAPTER FIVE

How to Become a Disciple
of Jesus (Christian)

The stated purpose of this book is to 'Meet God' or to explain and acquaint the reader with the God of the Bible. So many people have been denied knowledge and the experience of His love by a variety of entities and events. Not all this was done with evil intent, but regardless, it was done. Parents who do not know Jesus are unable to pass this knowledge and good news to their kids. Atheist, agnostics, and deniers of any higher power often denounce all religions and encourage the thought that mankind is the highest form of consciousness. People of other faiths worshipping inanimate objects, philosophies, Buddha, or the gods of Hinduism and Islam, etc.... are usually faithful to their beliefs, but they do not know the only true God—the God of the Bible. The celestial clock is ticking, and so many need to "Meet God."

With this and more in mind, the final section of this book will be a brief overview of how to become a Christian; to know God and His promises, to be saved, and to glorify God on earth while awaiting Jesus's return. Keep in mind this is brief and uncomplicated *but* of the utmost importance. Do not try to enter a relationship with God in a flippant or insincere state of mind. God knows our heart, and He is not "tricked" by empty words and dishonest actions. If you think someone else saying a prayer for you (not in the Bible) or getting baptized on a whim will equal salvation, please read the process described and compare the differences.

BECOME AWARE OF YOUR LOST CONDITION

Romans 5:12: "Therefore, just as sin came into the world through one man, and death through sin, and *so* death spread to all men because all sinned".

Romans 3:22-24: "The righteousness of God through faith in Jesus Christ for all who believe. For there is no distinction: for all have sinned and fall short of the glory of God, and are justified by his grace as a gift, through the redemption that is in Christ Jesus."

Luke 19:10: "For the Son of Man came to seek and to save the lost."

Much of Genesis 3 tells the story of sin entering the world and death being the consequence. Many other verses throughout the Bible tell of our death eternal if we do not consider our lost condition.

CHOOSE ETERNAL LIFE OVER DEATH ETERNAL

No one has to die in hell who does not want that end. We have the freewill to choose and change our lives accordingly.

Romans 6:20-23: "For when you were slaves of sin, you were free in regard to righteousness. But what fruit were you getting at that time from the things of which you are now ashamed? For the end of those things is death. But now that you have been set free from sin and have become slaves of God, the fruit you get leads to sanctification and its end, eternal life. For the wages of sin is death, but the free gift of God is eternal life in Christ Jesus our Lord."

We can choose life over death, Jesus over Satan, and heaven over hell. Now it is always a choice, but it entails commitment, not just a momentary impulse. Choosing life requires changes in priorities, focus, and deep self-examination. It requires effort and sacrifice, but the benefit is astounding and forever.

MEET JESUS

In person? Not yet. Jesus now resides with God, and His throne is to the right of the Father. But in Spirit, yes. We can meet Him through scripture such as the ones below and oh so many more. He can be shared by those who are His disciples by their changed lives and testimony. Good deeds done in His name testify loudly even as creation reflects His glory, but to really get to know Him, talk (pray) to Him and listen. Just as in John 17, Jesus talks to God, you can converse with Him through prayer; silently or loudly makes no difference.

John 17:1-8 When Jesus had spoken these words, he lifted up his eyes to heaven, and said, "Father, the hour has come; glorify your Son that the Son may glorify you, 2 since you have given him authority over all flesh, to give eternal life to all whom you have given him. 3 And this is eternal life, that they know you, the only true God, and Jesus Christ whom you have sent. 4 I glorified you on earth, having accomplished the work that you gave me to do. 5 And now, Father, glorify me in your own presence with the glory that I had with you before the world existed. 6 "I have manifested your name to the people whom you gave me out of the world. Yours they were, and you gave them to me, and they have kept your word. 7 Now they know that everything that you have given me is from you. 8 For I have given them the words that you gave me, and they have received them and have come to know in truth that I came from you; and they have believed that you sent me.

This chapter goes on to bless His disciples then and now. It has been called the "High Priestly Prayer" by centuries of anonymous Christians. Notice that in verses 6-8, the people who met and chose Him now know the truth.

2 Corinthians 5:16-21: "From now on, therefore, we regard no one according to the flesh. Even though we once regarded Christ according to the flesh, we regard him thus no longer. Therefore, if anyone is in Christ, he is a new creation. The old has died; behold, the new has come. All this is from God, who through Christ reconciled us to himself and gave us the ministry of reconciliation; that is, in Christ God was reconciling the world to himself, not counting their trespasses against them, and entrusting to us the message of reconciliation. Therefore, we are ambassadors for Christ, God making his appeal through us. We implore you on behalf of Christ,

be reconciled to God. For our sake he made him (Jesus) to be sin who knew no sin, so that in him we might become the righteousness of God."

Apostle Paul is telling the church in Corinth that those who follow Jesus are new creations spiritually. They are forgiven and restored to God's graces. Jesus made it possible as His evangelists like Paul are begging sinners to be saved through Jesus and become righteous. Meeting Jesus is most important as He is the way to God.

John 14:6: "Jesus said to him, 'I am the way, and the truth, and the life. No one comes to the Father except through me.'"

BELIEVE THAT JESUS CAN SAVE YOU

Many people question if Jesus can save them despite a past of sin and debauchery. Others question their worthiness. Many think they have waited too long. Low self-esteem, self-doubt, and a poor understanding of Jesus's love and willingness to save have left many in despair and others rejecting the premise of a loving God. The truth is that no one is beyond salvation who choose to be saved and does not turn back.

Acts 4:12: "And there is salvation in no one else, for there is no other name under heaven given among men by which we must be saved."

Titus 3:3-7: "For we ourselves were once foolish, disobedient, led astray, slaves to various passions and pleasures, passing our days in malice and envy, hated by others and hating one another. But when the goodness and loving-kindness of God our Savior appeared, he saved us, not because of works done by us in righteousness, but according to his own mercy, by the washing of regeneration and renewal of the Holy Spirit, whom he poured out on us richly through Jesus Christ our Savior, so that being justified by his grace we might become heirs according to the hope of eternal life."

Paul, in writing to Titus a young evangilist, reminds him that Jesus saved Christians when they were sinners and full of hate. It was through Jesus that the Holy Spirit was poured out on them and can be on you also.

TRUST AND BUILD FAITH IN
JESUS TO SAVE YOU

We are to pray for everyone as God wants all to be saved. That includes you!

1 Timothy 2:1-6: "First of all, then, I urge that supplications, prayers, intercessions, and thanksgivings be made for all people, for kings and all who are in high positions, that we may lead a peaceful and quiet life, godly and dignified in every way. This is good, and it is pleasing in the sight of God our Savior, who desires all people to be saved and to come to the knowledge of the truth. For there is one God, and there is one mediator between God and men, the man Christ Jesus, who gave himself as a ransom for all, which is the testimony given at the proper time."

1 Timothy 4:6-9: "If you put these things before the brothers, you will be a good servant of Christ Jesus, being trained in the words of the faith and of the good doctrine that you have followed. Have nothing to do with irreverent, silly myths. Rather train yourself for godliness; for while bodily training is of some value, godliness is of value in every way, as it holds promise for the present life and also for the life to come. The saying is trustworthy and deserving of full acceptance."

Training ourselves for Godliness helps now and eternally. Trust in this. Enoch (Gen. 5) had faith and trust in God. God made an exception in the normal life cycle for him.

Hebrews 11:5-6: "By faith Enoch was taken up so that he should not see death, and he was not found, because God had taken him. Now before he was taken he was commended as having pleased God. And without faith it is impossible to please him, for whoever would draw near to God must believe that he exists and that he rewards those who seek him."

John 3:16-18: "For God so loved the world, that he gave his only Son, that whoever believes in him should not perish but have eternal life. For God did not send his Son into the world to condemn the world, but in order that the world might be saved through him. Whoever believes in him is not condemned, but whoever does not believe is condemned already, because he has not believed in the name of the only Son of God."

Repent of the Past and Seek Forgiveness

AS we trust and build faith, it shows sincerity and love toward God. As such, the next choice is, do I continue living as I have, or do I turn 180 degrees from the old life of sin? Repentance is an action, belief, emotion, and spiritual declaration. We leave a life of sin and worldly pleasures and allow Jesus to transform our lives. We believe and choose selflessness over selfishness by loving God and others as ourselves, we develop compassion for the lost around us, and finally, we view life as a spiritual being, seeking to honor and praise God the Creator.

Luke 15:3-7: "So he told them this parable: 'What man of you, having a hundred sheep, if he has lost one of them, does not leave the ninety-nine in the open country, and go after the one that is lost, until he finds it? And when he has found it, he lays it on his shoulders, rejoicing. And when he comes home, he calls together his friends and his neighbors, saying to them, "Rejoice with me, for I have found my sheep that was lost." 7 Just so, I tell you, there will be more joy in heaven over one sinner who repents than over ninety and nine righteous persons who need no repentance.'"

This parable that Jesus told in Luke emphasizes how much the celestial beings rejoice over sinners who repent. Jesus did not come for the righteous but for the lost.

1 John 1:5-10: "This is the message we have heard from him and proclaim to you, that God is light, and in him is no darkness at all. If we say we have fellowship with him while we walk in darkness, we lie and do not practice the truth. But if we walk in the light, as he is in the light, we have fellowship with one another, and the blood of Jesus his Son cleanses us from all sin. If we say we have no sin, we deceive ourselves, and the truth is not in us. If we confess our sins, he is faithful and just to forgive us our sins and to cleanse us from all unrighteousness. If we say we have not sinned, we make him a liar, and his word is not in us."

CONFESS JESUS AS GOD'S SON AND SUBMIT TO HIM AS LORD OF YOUR LIFE

In several passages given below, the emphasis is on confessing Jesus as the Messiah, Christ, Son of God, Lord, and Savior. As such, we must either confess Him on earth and live the transformed life of a Christian or in heaven to our God on Judgment Day while He reviews all our unforgiven sins. Easy choice.

Matthew 16:13-17: "Now when Jesus came into the district of Caesarea Philippi, he asked his disciples, 'Who do people say that the Son of Man is?' And they said, 'Some say John the Baptist, others say Elijah, and others Jeremiah or one of the prophets.' He said to them, 'But who do you say that I am?' Simon Peter replied, 'You are the Christ, the Son of the living God.' And Jesus answered him, 'Blessed are you, Simon Bar-Jonah! For flesh and blood has not revealed this to you, but my Father who is in heaven.'"

1 John 4:13-16: "By this we know that we abide in him and he in us, because he has given us of his Spirit. And we have seen and testify that the Father has sent his Son to be the Savior of the world. Whoever confesses that Jesus is the Son of God, God abides in him, and he in God. So we have come to know and to believe the love that God has for us. God is love, and whoever abides in love abides in God, and God abides in him."

Philippians 2:8-11: "And being found in human form, he humbled himself by becoming obedient to the point of death, even death on a cross. Therefore God has highly exalted him and bestowed on him the name that is above every name, so that at the name of Jesus every knee should bow, in heaven and on earth and under the earth, and every tongue confess that Jesus Christ is Lord, to the glory of God the Father."

Romans 10:6-10: "But the righteousness based on faith says, "Do not say in your heart, 'Who will ascend into heaven?'" (that is, to bring Christ down) "or 'Who will descend into the abyss?'" (that is, to bring Christ up from the dead). But what does it say? "The word is near you, in your mouth and in your heart" (that is, the word of faith that we proclaim); because, if you confess with your mouth that Jesus is Lord and believe in your heart that God raised him from the dead, you will be saved. For with the heart one believes and is justified, and with the mouth one confesses and is saved".

Be Baptized (Immersion in Water)

In every story of conversion told in the book of Acts, starting in chapter 2, the lost person/people were baptized as part of their salvation. Jesus was baptized by John the Baptist "to fulfill all righteousness" (Matthew 3). In John 4, Jesus's disciples baptized believers in the Jordan River. In the great commission, as stated in Matthew 28:16-20, Jesus instructed His disciples, "Now the eleven disciples went to Galilee, to the mountain to which Jesus had directed them. And when they saw him they worshipped him, but some doubted. And Jesus came and said to them, 'All authority in heaven and on earth has been given to me. Go therefore and make disciples of all nations, baptizing them in the name of the Father and of the Son and of the Holy Spirit, teaching them to observe all that I have commanded you. And behold, I am with you always, to the end of the age.'"

Jesus required baptism from all who believed and wanted salvation. Please ignore the thief-on-the-cross argument. At the moment, Jesus granted paradise to this man; he was still in the last moments of the old law. Christ came to fulfill it as no mortal could do so. Once He is resurrected and gains victory over death, the new covenant begins. As an exception to the rule—it is only an exception—it does not change the sum of scripture in the new kingdom. There is no promise or hint that He will ever do it again, whereas there is plenty of text to convince an honest person that baptism is required. Denial of this indicates a rebellious spirit.

Acts 2:37-38: "Now when they heard this they were cut to the heart, and said to Peter and the rest of the apostles, 'Brothers, what shall we do?' And Peter said to them, 'Repent and be baptized every one of you in the name of Jesus Christ for the forgiveness of your sins, and you will receive the gift of the Holy Spirit.'"

In that passage, Peter has shared the good news of Jesus, and many in the crowd suddenly see their part in Jesus's death. In answer to their question of "what to do," Peter tells them of baptism for remission of sins and receipt of the Holy Spirit.

1 Peter 3:21-22: "Baptism, which corresponds to this, now saves you, not as a removal of dirt from the body but as an appeal to God for a good conscience, through the resurrection of Jesus Christ, who has gone into

heaven and is at the right hand of God, with angels, authorities, and powers having been subjected to him."

Baptism is more than removal of soil; it reflects our good conscience to God. It shows obedience. It emulates Jesus example and fulfills His command.

Receive the Indwelling
of the Holy Spirit

Fifty days after Jesus was crucified, the apostles were gathered in Jerusalem, where they received the Holy Spirit promised by Jesus. In Acts 2, Peter and the others preached the gospel to the people gathered there (twelve nations represented). They outlined the life of Jesus and laid the guilt at the feet of those responsible for killing the Messiah. In shock, they asked, "What do we do?" His response is recorded below:

Acts 2:38-41: "And Peter said to them, 'Repent and be baptized every one of you in the name of Jesus Christ for the forgiveness of your sins, and you will receive the gift of the Holy Spirit. For the promise is for you and for your children and for all who are far off, everyone whom the Lord our God calls to himself.' And with many other words he bore witness and continued to exhort them, saying, 'Save yourselves from this crooked generation.' So those who received his word were baptized, and there were added that day about three thousand souls."

Notice the close proximity of baptism and receiving the Holy Spirit. Notice the promise. It was not only for those who heard Peter that day, but it is still happening today. Two things happened: People who heard the word and were baptized received the Holy Spirit and were added to the church.

Saul was a devout Jew who persecuted Jesus's disciples, often arresting, and hauling them to Jewish leaders for punishment or worse. Jesus struck him blind as he traveled to Damascus to arrest others. After three days of blindness, Ananias, a man of God, was sent to him as seen below:

Acts 9:17-19: "So Ananias departed and entered the house. And laying his hands on him he said, 'Brother Saul, the Lord Jesus who appeared to you on the road by which you came has sent me so that you may regain your sight and be filled with the Holy Spirit.' And immediately something like scales fell from his eyes, and he regained his sight. Then he rose and was baptized; and taking food, he was strengthened."

Peter was called by God to preach Jesus to the Gentiles (non-Jewish people) in Acts 10. Near the end of this sermon, the ones who believed acted accordingly.

Acts 10:42-48: "And he (Jesus) commanded us to preach to the people and to testify that he is the one appointed by God to be judge of the living and the dead. To him all the prophets bear witness that everyone who believes in him receives forgiveness of sins through his name." While Peter was still saying these things, the Holy Spirit fell on all who heard the word. And the believers from among the circumcised who had come with Peter were amazed, because the gift of the Holy Spirit was poured out even on the Gentiles. For they were hearing them speaking in tongues and extolling God. Then Peter declared, 'Can anyone withhold water for baptizing these people, who have received the Holy Spirit just as we have?' And he commanded them to be baptized in the name of Jesus Christ. Then they asked him to remain for some days."

As stated earlier, those people who were converted by the apostles received the Holy Spirit either just before or just after baptism. This writer has taught several people the gospel in the last thirty years. Most asked to be baptized, and you could often see the fruit of the Holy Spirit soon after this was done. I have had one person tell me that she was saved prior to baptism but did not feel "right" until she was later baptized. Who am I to question God's timing?

GROW AND BE TRANSFORMED

Many authors would stop at receive the Holy Spirit, thinking, okay, they are now saved. At the moment, they are, but just because Jesus calls us as we are does not mean He wants us to remain that way. No, just the opposite. He wants us to confirm our changes by becoming holy. Jesus wants us to grow in Spirit, truth, faith, and love. He wants us to become as much like Him as we can. In the Old Testament, God repeatedly challenged people to "be Holy, as I am Holy" (Leviticus 11:44,45; 19:2; 20:7, 26; 21:8). Likewise, Jesus wants us to grow and be transformed. As we grow, the body of Christ (church) also grows.

Romans 12:1-2: "I appeal to you therefore, brothers, by the mercies of God, to present your bodies as a living sacrifice, holy and acceptable to God, which is your spiritual worship. Do not be conformed to this world, but be transformed by the renewal of your mind, that by testing you may discern what is the will of God, what is good and acceptable and perfect."

"By testing" gives the sense that we may not always get it right the first time, although in time we develop the discernment of what is and is not God's will. This hastened by regular bible study and prayer.

2 Corinthians 3:16-18: "But when one turns to the Lord, the veil is removed. Now the Lord is the Spirit, and where the Spirit of the Lord is, there is freedom. And we all, with unveiled face, beholding the glory of the Lord, are being transformed into the same image from one degree of glory to another. For this comes from the Lord who is the Spirit."

Another way we are transformed is by boldly seeking God and His glory. As we do, the transformation God desires happens among Christians.

MAKE DISCIPLES

As Jesus died to save mankind from sin, Christians, die to self, in order to bring others to Jesus. Hoarding salvation is not loving God, loving your neighbor, or loving the church as Jesus did. This requires not only the growth mentioned above, but also the boldness to share Jesus with others.

In Matthew 28:18-20, Jesus empowers the apostles and, by extension, Christians today to seek the lost: "And Jesus came and said to them, 'All authority in heaven and on earth has been given to me. Go therefore and make disciples of all nations, baptizing them in the name of the Father and of the Son and of the Holy Spirit, teaching them to observe all that I have commanded you. And behold, I am with you always, to the end of the age.'"

In his letter to the Romans, Paul stresses the importance of preaching the word. If you wish to offer Jesus to others, one way is by preaching or teaching. Using scripture is an immensely powerful method.

Romans 10:14-17: "How then will they call on him in whom they have not believed? And how are they to believe in him of whom they have never heard? And how are they to hear without someone preaching? And how are they to preach unless they are sent? As it is written, 'How beautiful are the feet of those who preach the good news!' But they have not all obeyed the gospel. For Isaiah says, 'Lord, who has believed what he has heard from us?' So faith comes from hearing, and hearing through the word of Christ."

1 Peter 2:9-12: "But you are a chosen race, a royal priesthood, a holy nation, a people for his own possession, that you may proclaim the excellencies of him who called you out of darkness into his marvelous light. Once you were not a people, but now you are God's people; once you had not received mercy, but now you have received mercy. Beloved, I urge you as sojourners and exiles to abstain from the passions of the flesh, which wage war against your soul. Keep your conduct among the Gentiles honorable, so that when they speak against you as evildoers, they may see your good deeds and glorify God on the day of visitation."

As this priesthood, we are to proclaim Jesus. Note the method here is by honorable living. Not everyone has the gift or teaching, but all of us can live the example of Jesus in everyday life. Express concern for the lost. Show compassion for those who struggle. Feed the poor. Visit the sick. Provide care for the parentless child or the ailing widow. I know people who make prayer their ministry. Others bake or cook food for those who are alone or grieving. There is no end to the ways in which we can reflect Jesus to others and gain an opportunity to share what He has done for us.

GLORIFY GOD

The ongoing obligation and opportunity all Christians work toward is glorifying God. The Three-in-One who created us, nurtured us, and provided life in abundance deserves to be glorified, praised, honored. As the four living creatures praise Him unendingly, and as the Old Testament writers repeatedly praised God, Christ followers need to act in a similar fashion.

1 Chronicles 16:23-27: "Sing to the Lord, all the earth! Tell of his salvation from day to day. Declare his glory among the nations, his marvelous works among all the peoples! For great is the Lord, and greatly to be praised, and he is to be feared above all gods. For all the gods of the peoples are worthless idols, but the Lord made the heavens. Splendor and majesty are before him; strength and joy are in his place."

1 Peter 4:10-11: "As each has received a gift, use it to serve one another, as good stewards of God's varied grace: whoever speaks, as one who speaks oracles of God; whoever serves, as one who serves by the strength that God supplies— in order that in everything God may be glorified through Jesus Christ. To him belong glory and dominion forever and ever. Amen."

God deserves our praise and merits all glory. He is the great "I Am," eternal, loving, compassionate, long-suffering, just, and merciful. As the "Doxology" # says,

Praise God from whom all blessings flow.
Praise Him, all creatures here below.
Praise Him above, ye heavenly host.
Praise Father, Son, and Holy Ghost.
Let me add, in Jesus's name, Amen.

Abbreviations of the Books of the Bible

Old Testament

Genesis	Gen.
Exodus	Ex.
Leviticus	Lev.
Numbers	Num.
Deuteronomy	Deut.
Joshua	Josh.
Judges	Judg.
Ruth	Ruth
1 Samuel	1 Sam.
2 Samuel	2 Sam.
1 Kings	1 Kings
2 Kings	2 Kings
1 Chronicles	1 Chron.
2 Chronicles	2 Chron.
Ezra	Ezra
Nehemiah	Neh.
Esther	Est.
Job	Job

Psalms	Ps.
Proverbs	Prov.
Ecclesiastes	Eccles.
Song of Solomon	Song
Isaiah	Isa.
Jeremiah	Jer.
Lamentations	Lam.
Ezekiel	Ezek.
Daniel	Dan.
Hosea	Hos.
Joel	Joel
Amos	Amos
Obadiah	Obad.
Jonah	Jonah
Micah	Mic.
Nahum	Nah.
Habakkuk	Hab.
Zephaniah	Zeph.
Haggai	Hag.
Zechariah	Zech.
Malachi	Mal.

New Testament

Matthew	Matt.
Mark	Mark
Luke	Luke
John	John
Acts	Acts
Romans	Rom.
1 Corinthians	1 Cor.

2 Corinthians	2 Cor.
Galatians	Gal.
Ephesians	Eph.
Philippians	Phil.
Colossians	Col.
1 Thessalonians	1 Thess.
2 Thessalonians	2 Thess.
1 Timothy	1 Tim.
2 Timothy	2 Tim.
Titus	Titus
Philemon	Philem.
Hebrews	Heb.
James	James
1 Peter	1 Pet.
2 Peter	2 Pet.
1 John	1 John
2 John	2 John
3 John	3 John
Jude	Jude
Revelation	Rev.

References

BOB GOFF. 2012. "LOVE DOES: DISCOVER A SECRETLY INCREIBLE LIFE IN AN ORDINARY WORLD". Thomas Nelson. Nashville, TN.

R.C. Sproul, 1988. The Holiness of God; Revised and Expanded by Tyndall House Publishers, Inc., Carol Stream, IL.

Howard, Alton H. Editor. 1994, "Songs of Faith and Praise, "Trust and Obey", 1887 by Sammis, J.H. Towner, D.B., p. 915, Howard Publishing Co, West Monroe, LA.

Airplane, Directed by Abrahams, Jim, Zucker, David, Zucker, Jerry 1984. Released by Paramount, Los Angeles, CA.

"The Battle Belongs to the Lord", by Jamie Owens-Collins, 1985 Fairhill Music, Inc.

John Piper,1984. "Beyond Forgiveness: Blasphemy Against the Spirit" desiringGod.org

Howard, Alton H. Editor. 1994, Songs of Faith and Praise, "Doxology" Ken, Thomas,1864, and Kocher, Conrad, 1838, (adapted Monk, William H.,1861), p. 66, Howard Publishing Co, West Monroe, LA.

Abbreviations, adapted from "The Holy Bible", English Standard Version (ESV), Text Edition 2011, Published by Crossway, Wheaton, IL. 60187 USA

Lightning Source UK Ltd.
Milton Keynes UK
UKHW011841280121
377874UK00008B/439/J